YOU END UP WHERE YOU'RE HEADING

YOU END UP WHERE YOU'RE HEADING

THE HIDDEN DANGERS OF LIVING A SAFE LIFE

JIMMY REX & CAMERON CARLING

HOUNDSTOOTH
PRESS

YOU END UP WHERE YOU'RE HEADING
The Hidden Dangers of Living a Safe Life

ISBN   978-1-5445-0920-4 *Hardcover*
       978-1-5445-0919-8 *Paperback*
       978-1-5445-0918-1 *Ebook*
       978-1-5445-1492-5 *Audiobook*

YOU END UP WHERE YOU'RE HEADING

THE HIDDEN DANGERS OF
LIVING A SAFE LIFE

JIMMY REX &
CAMERON CARLING

HOUNDSTOOTH
PRESS

YOU END UP WHERE YOU'RE HEADING

The Hidden Dangers of Living a Safe Life

ISBN   978-1-5445-0920-4 *Hardcover*

978-1-5445-0919-8 *Paperback*

978-1-5445-0918-1 *Ebook*

978-1-5445-1492-5 *Audiobook*

CONTENTS

PROLOGUE

TWO POTENTIAL PATHS

PATH ONE

When the alarm goes off, you can't believe it's morning. Another day you're not ready to face. You check your phone, pushing aside the book you've been meaning to read on your nightstand. Your feet haven't hit the floor yet and your boss is already yelling at you through email. Why do you keep going back?

After a rushed breakfast and too little time with your family, you're on the road for the thirty-minute commute to the office. As you hit the freeway on-ramp, all you can see are brake lights. Thirty minutes turns into ninety. You go from sitting in your car to sitting at your desk. More email. The picture next to your monitor of you and your friends at Yellowstone reminds you that you still haven't gone to a national park in all fifty states. After the baby, you got stalled at twelve. And then it was hard to get vacation. And the flights to Alaska are so expensive. Maybe next year.

You crack open the single-use plastic containing your lunch. The turkey sandwich is drier than usual, so you settle for the chips. The guy next to you on the park bench is sweating profusely, his shirt sticking to his chest. You've lost your appetite. Back to the car. Sit. Back at your desk. Sit. Afternoon staff meeting. Sit. Your boss asks a question but it's more of a directive, "Can you have the quarterly report done by end of day?"

The call home that you'd be late was received icier than usual. There's barely enough time to do all the yardwork let alone have a date night. Back in the car. Sit. All the lights seem to be on in the house as you pull into the driveway. The mortgage was more than you could afford, let alone the electricity bill, but interest rates were so low, your dad said you'd be crazy not to go bigger. You look up and down the empty streets. Everyone inside, safe and sound. It's Wednesday. Spaghetti night. Again.

PATH TWO

You're already awake when they knock on your door. You lock eyes with your mission lead, and he gives you a confident nod. You're only a few steps out the door of your

Mexican border-town motel when the beachside drug pusher offers you weed. You decline; you're looking for underage girls instead. But he's got you covered for that too, you just need to find boss Carlos. The adrenaline is building in your body. It's good to be back.

You rushed out without breakfast, but undercover missions rarely follow a schedule. You were supposed to meet Carlos thirty minutes ago, but it's turned into ninety. You can't sit down; the alley you're standing in is covered in urine and garbage. A black SUV with dark tinted windows pulls up and the brake lights engage. Two armed guards emerge who seem like they shouldn't have even fit inside. You're scared, but the thought of having a successful rescue calms you down.

Your stomach growls as the negotiation for the "party" drags on. You're thankful for the Spanish you learned on a previous mission as you haggle over the price per girl and the preferred location to make it seem legit. The guy standing across from you, an ex-Navy SEAL, briefly touches his shirt. You pray they don't see any of the hidden cameras. Carlos asks you a question, but it's more of an invitation, "Can you be back in two weeks?"

The night arrives and Carlos parades the forty girls into the room. All the lights are dimmed. You're standing next to a handful of Special Forces guys in bad Hawaiian shirts.

When the code word drops and you get "arrested" along with Carlos and his crew, you revel in their surprised faces. Every one of those girls, safe and sound. It's a Thursday or Friday, but it doesn't matter. A few hours later, you hop on a plane back to the States, excited for what challenges the next day might hold.

Two paths. Which one makes you feel more alive?

INTRODUCTION

WHERE THE TWO PATHS DIVERGED

THE SETTLER AND THE EXPLORER

You've probably heard of Ferdinand Magellan, Vasco da Gama, and Marco Polo. These famous explorers set out on ambitious journeys to discover new worlds, pulled by the promise of foreign riches and fame, and made it back to tell the tale. But what about Percy Fawcett? Gaspar and Miguel Corte-Real? They don't ring a bell? It's because they disappeared, following the washed-away footsteps of most explorers before them. History hasn't been kind to exploration: disease, brutal conflicts, harsh environments, poor nutrition, not to mention the incomplete or inaccurate maps they had to follow. Even Magellan, killed in battle in the Philippines, and da Gama, who died of malaria, eventually ran out of luck. When a ship left port, everyone aboard knew they weren't likely to return.

What explorers left behind were the settlers. These were the people who built walls around the places already mapped. Their job was to tame the "discovered" lands and make them predictable, destroy diversity, and eliminate surprise. It was a life dedicated to toil and slow expansion, never venturing too far off the beaten path for fear of what lurked beyond. They held down the proverbial or literal fort, tilled the fields, reproduced, and warned the next generation of the dangers beyond the walls. Settlers traded a life of discovery for a more certain existence, a safer anonymity. When the castle doors were closed at night, everyone inside knew it was the best chance they had at survival.

But times have changed.

Social and technological advances have all but wiped out the dangers of the frontier. Calories are cheap, transportation is safe and fast, and the plagues of years past have been all but eradicated (not many cases of scurvy these days). Modern-day explorers can venture out with a high degree of certainty, knowing they'll return in one piece. Entrepreneurial explorers can launch an armada of online products without risking their lives. Scientific explorers can make bold claims and discoveries without being accused of witchcraft or heresy. The sailing is undoubtedly smoother.

But modern-day settlers? They're the ones in danger. Instead of protecting their inhabitants, the settlement walls are now unnecessarily confining and restricting. Today's settlers have moved past a safe predictability and into a crisis of complacency. They aren't surviving by staying put; they're slowly dying in their office chairs and heated car seats. The well-worn path has paved right over their dreams and higher callings. The small cuts of apathy aren't outward killers, but they drain the life out, nonetheless. The harsh conditions have moved out of the frontier and settled into our bodies and minds in the form of addiction, obesity, burnout, heart disease, anxiety, and depression. And for what reward? The biggest house? Lackluster relationships? Comfort?

The fates of Explorers and Settlers hit an inflection point long ago, but we didn't update our cultural narratives or mental maps. The change was so subtle and incremental that we failed to adapt. Instead, we continue our steady diet of well-intentioned advice telling us to stay within the settlement for safety. We blindly follow the outdated risk meters of our brains to a life of lesser rewards. We trust but don't verify. Yet, it's not too late to open your eyes to today's landscape and redraw the maps. It's not too late to see what happened and change course. Exploration is within your grasp.

The joy of exploring is something humans have always known. We're born Explorers, innately drawn to test the boundaries of our world, to pick up the things we come across and turn them over in our hands with wonder. It's in our core to ask, "What if..." and follow our curiosity. And only through an ill-fitted modern "education" are we taught to be Settlers. We're lined up in rows and drilled to rinse and repeat and regurgitate. The difficult task of today is to *unlearn* what we've been taught—to debunk the belief system that tells us exploring is inherently dangerous and settling is safe. The world and culture that rewarded settlers is long gone.

This book is for the buried Explorer in all of us. For the apathetic Explorer, whose dull comforts are barely outpacing the pain. For the fearful Explorer, held back by the anxiety of the unknown. For the lost Explorer, who started down the path but met resistance along the way. The following chapters will unfold the updated map of our changed world and plot the course for a modern way of exploration. But it's up to you to take the first step, or you'll be left holding down the fort while someone else discovers the world. As Lao Tzu said, "If you do not change direction, you might end up where you are heading."

EXPLORERS AMONG US

So who am I to set things straight? When you think of an Explorer, you likely don't picture a real estate agent from Utah, but that's what I've been doing for the past fifteen years and where I've lived all my life. I grew up in a family of seven kids and quickly learned it wasn't in my best interest to settle. If you weren't on top of things when Mom came home from grocery shopping, you were getting the scraps. We weren't poor, but we definitely didn't have any extra. If I wanted something other than school clothes or sports equipment, I had to figure out a way to get it on my own. Garage sales, hanging Christmas lights, buying and selling concert tickets—I was always hustling. I even learned the core tenet of investing, buy low and sell high, by searching out discount toys at one store and then "returning" them for store credit at another store that still had the toy at regular price. When my high school baseball coach challenged us to sell ten T-shirts to raise money for a team trip, I sold 157. I thought I needed to prove something to the coach, so settling wasn't going to cut it.

When it was time for me to head out on my own, I'd already been wired the opposite of most people—settling scared the hell out of me. I was more afraid of dying with an unchecked bucket list than I was of kicking the bucket while checking them off. In my mind, I *was* following the safe path by squeezing the most out of life while I was still breathing. Leaving anything on the table seemed risky. I simply followed my heart and figured it out along the way. I built successful businesses but also had my life savings destroyed by bad investments. I went on a church mission to Mexico to baptize the unenlightened to my faith and returned years later on a humanitarian mission to liberate child slaves from their captors. I've swum with sharks, jumped off cliffs, and run with the bulls. There was huge upside and little downside to pushing the boundaries of the world around me. And even if something went wrong, I always knew there was pizza in the trunk. Stay with me; it makes sense, I promise.

One of my favorite movies growing up was *Tommy Boy*, starring Chris Farley and David Spade. Farley is the hapless heir to a struggling automotive parts company, and Spade is the straight man trying to keep him out of trouble as they hit the road on a last-ditch sales trip to save the company. After a particularly bad afternoon, they find themselves at a restaurant trying to regroup. The kitchen is closed until dinner, but Farley is determined to order chicken wings. He launches into a crazy monologue in hopes the unrelenting waitress will see the world like he does. It's bizarre and vulnerable and a little bit scary. And it works. Spade is dumbfounded and wants to know why he can't sell like that in front of customers. What Farley says has replayed in the back of my head ever since:

> "I'm just having fun. If we didn't get the wings, so what? We still got that meat-lovers' pizza in the trunk."

If I went after something in my life and I didn't get it, the worst-case scenario was the life I already had (the pizza in the trunk). The best-case scenario was the thing I wanted (delicious wings!). Where other people saw risk, I saw nothing to lose. Where other people saw a straight path, I saw exciting paths in every direction. I wanted to live, not just exist.

As I expanded my world beyond the walls of high school and college and the borders of my home state of Utah, I came across other kindred spirits who believed they had nothing to lose as well. I built a network of people who seemed to have a never-ending supply of pizza in the trunk. They already knew how standard life tasted, so they were constantly pushing to get the kitchen open when everyone else said it was closed. They pushed the boundaries of their bodies, they pushed the reach of their ideas, and they pushed the limits of their spirits. It was a secret society who discovered the key to living a full and expansive life.

I started a podcast, *The Jimmy Rex Show* [1], because I thought the stories I'd heard needed to be told firsthand and it seemed wrong to keep this wisdom to myself. I bought some microphones, called up my friends, and hit record. I had no idea what I was doing and the horrible audio on the first couple of episodes made that clear. But as the interviews piled up, I knew I was onto something. No matter where a story unfolded—the baseball diamond, the hair salon, or the cramped offices of struggling entrepreneurs—it followed a common arc. My podcast guests weren't a bunch of risk-seeking anomalies but a group with a shared mindset and a limitless path they all seemed to be following. They felt safe to explore, knowing the downsides were limited. But how did this group of people, myself included, escape the settlement while so many others were still stuck behind the walls?

WHEN SETTLING FEELS SAFER

The conditions that create Explorers, or turn them into Settlers, are well-studied areas. Two twentieth-century scholars in particular were experts in exploration. One was a mythologist, who spent a lifetime examining history's greatest journeys (the path of the Explorer). The other was a psychologist, who dedicated his career to understanding human motivation and the drives that propel people forward or hold them back (the psychopathology of the Explorer). Together, they complete the picture on how to live a full life through exploring your personal potential.

Abraham Maslow (1908–1970) was an American psychologist and a sought-after professor at Columbia, Brooklyn College, and Brandeis. Maslow was a leader in the positive psychology movement, a focus on mental health rather than mental illness, and believed strongly in the potential of humanity. He was best known for his hierarchy of needs, a theory of psychological health focused on the fulfillment of five common human needs—physiological (e.g., food and water), safety, love and belonging, esteem, and self-actualization (i.e., reaching your peak potential). If someone was severely deficient in a lower-level need, Maslow claimed, it was almost impossible for them to fulfill, or even consider fulfilling, a higher-level need. For example, if someone was worried about their personal safety on a regular basis, they wouldn't be capable of pursuing their talent and passion for art.

In addition to needs, Maslow also believed we are propelled forward in life by delight. "Growth takes place when the next step forward is subjectively more delightful, more joyous, more intrinsically satisfying than the last; that the only way we can ever know what is right for us is that it feels better subjectively than any alternative" [2]. He thought the key struggle of our lives was a never-ending series of choices between "the delights of safety and growth, dependence and independence, regression and progression, immaturity and maturity." If safety feels better, that's what we choose. If safety feels less desirable or even dangerous, we opt for growth.

I'm sure if Maslow were to examine the Settlers of today, he'd say their safety was more than sufficient but the delight associated with growth was low. When faced with a choice of fulfilling a higher-level need or stockpiling safety nets, most are choosing the latter. When there's a clear and desirable path forward—high school to college, yellow belt to green belt, manager to regional manager—progression happens willingly. But when the pavement abruptly stops and the road signs disappear? The choice between safety and growth isn't so clear. When you hit the border walls of your life and see the uncertainty beyond, you stop; the risk of the unknown feels too great. It's a bit like starting a hike and seeing this sign at the trailhead:

> **Path One:** Everyone is doing it, no big surprises. The trail is flat and wide, no rocks to speak of. DO NOT go off the path for any reason. It's basically the same every time you do it. Three miles.

> **Path Two:** Rarely traveled, gets hard at some point but we're not sure for how long. There might be someone or something dangerous partway through. It could go on forever without a way to get back. Return rate unknown. Have you heard about Path One?

Path Two doesn't stand a chance. And that's when you settle. You settle into an identity ("Market Researcher" or "Middle-Aged"), you settle into ways of thinking ("bad with numbers" or "good with kids"), and you settle into routines (the "tradition" of watching eight hours of football on Sundays). You could walk through your life with your eyes closed. And you do.

Those trail signs are exactly the inner dialogue we have with ourselves when faced with a choice between settling and exploring. "I'm a great mom, but I don't know anything about starting a business," "I want to sign up for a marathon, but I hear the training is brutal," "I want to go into sales, but I'm not outgoing." The delight of something new can't overcome the perceived risk. Back to the grind, stay put, sit down. But the result is not contentment; it's a gnawing restlessness that won't go away. Each passing day is an ever-widening gap between what you hoped for in life and what you settled on. You'll take the same vacation, order the pad thai again, and stay in the job that "pays the bills." Why? Because it's the smart play. The safe play. Going out on your own is dangerous. So you settle. Down.

What I learned from my podcast guests and from examining my own life, was the Maslow antidote for settling—yielding to uncertainty to unlock the delight. Fifty years before the invention of the iPhone, Maslow could see the pace of technological advancement would require humanity to change in fundamental ways. He believed we would need to "make ourselves over into the people who don't need to staticize the world, who don't need to freeze it and make it stable, who don't need to do what their daddies did, who are able confidently to face tomorrow not knowing what's going to come" [3]. When you embrace the uncertainty, you allow yourself to see the delight instead of just the danger. When you accept that you can't freeze the world into something safe and stable, you can put your full focus on the delight of growth. And with those new eyes, the sign at the trailhead (and your inner dialogue) will look like this:

> **Path Two:** This path is made for you! It's going to seem a bit scary at first, but you'll get over it and eventually embrace the novelty. The middle is hard as hell, but you'll feel amazing when you get through it. At some point, you're going to see a cave. DO NOT pass up this opportunity to explore some deeper truths about yourself. Back on the main trail, you'll see an enormous mountain. Climb it. You can do it. At the top, you'll find an incredible reward but probably not what you expected. This trail is as long as you need it to be. Repeat visits will never be the same. Enjoy.

How could you pass up Path Two?! You can always come back safely behind the walls of the settlement, but you can never find the riches beyond if you stay within them. The delightful path of the Explorer will be opened up and you'll be drawn to the thing you previously feared. As Maslow put it, you will have recovered "the ability to perceive one's own delights," someone who "enjoys change, who is able to improvise." But which way should you go?

DELIGHT WITH DIRECTION

Joseph Campbell (1904–1987) was a professor at Sarah Lawrence College in New York, and one of the most influential figures in comparative mythology and modern storytelling.

His groundbreaking work, *The Hero with a Thousand Faces* (1949), describes the familiar arc found in all world myths of adventure, personal change, and a triumphant return. It's a thread you can find in epic poems (Homer's *Odyssey*) and epic space operas (*Star Wars*). Campbell named this ageless path of the seeker the Hero's Journey.

The appeal and familiarity of the Hero's Journey is widespread because of the core human issues it deals with. It's the fear of facing the unknown and overcoming failure. It's building on small wins and the necessity of joining with other people to accomplish incredible feats. And ultimately, it's the riches of personal growth that outshine the treasure initially sought. Campbell saw this cyclical journey as the secret to life: "People say that what we're all seeking is a meaning for life. I don't think that's what we're really seeking. I think that what we're seeking is an experience of being alive" [4].

Although his work focused on legend and lore, Campbell knew the learnings could (and should) be applied to the paths taken by real people. Where Maslow knew why we find it hard to leave the settlement, Campbell understood what we'd find on the frontier. Campbell's Hero's Journey framework has been used widely by creators of fictional worlds, but I wanted to make it accessible for the world we live in. A hero is the mythical idea of someone born different than us, endowed by the gods at birth and given divine assistance along the way. But you and I are human, a mortal bundle of flaws. We're ordinary Explorers who have to develop and draw out our greatness; it isn't handed to us. We struggle and hit dead ends and don't always get what we set out to find but often get what we need. I wanted to cut from the same cloth as the Hero's Journey but end up with something an everyday person, flaws and all, could follow. Mythical heroes need providence; Explorers need a plan.

CHARTING YOUR PATH

Building on Campbell's map and Maslow's mindset, I created my own system for the process of rediscovering your inner Explorer. It breaks down into four phases:

1. **CH**anging Your Mind
2. **A**dapting Your Body
3. **R**evealing Your Heart
4. **T**ransmitting Your Soul

The **C.H.A.R.T.** framework is the continuous cycle of choosing growth over safety, creating new habits, accepting and integrating who you've become, and sharing what you've learned along the way. This will become a familiar loop you'll travel throughout your life, and as long as you remain committed to the forward progress of exploration, this path will never lead you astray.

Ultimately, we're not afraid of hard things; we're afraid of uncertainty. My hope with this book, and this framework, is to help remove the uncertainty of Path Two, the Explorer's path. The following chapters will explore the nuance of each step and introduce you to extraordinary modern Explorers who are following the path today. These are real people who came to the end of their settlements (refugee, drug addict, single mom, failure) and chose the endless road of growth instead of accepting their fate. They pushed beyond the walls constructed by their cultures, faiths, and family to reveal the joy of continuously discovering their own potential.

Explorers' lives are built on investigation and becoming more familiar with themselves and the world. There are no limits on exploration, no ceilings, and no wrong answers. Obstacles become observations. Ambiguity becomes adventure. The only expectation of an Explorer is movement, with the gap between what they want and what they get closed with every step. Explorers can't walk through life with their eyes closed because they're not always sure what's ahead. They're open and awake to every possibility, and you can be, too.

But a word of caution: "A map is not the territory it represents" [5]. There are limits to any model, and the world is not as simple as "Follow These 10 Easy Steps to Succeed." Real life is full of experiences that happen well outside the bounds of any framework. The circumstances of your life (your territory) may not come in the same order as they're laid out in the book (the map). Life isn't order; it's a mess. A twisting, turning, beautiful mess. So when you look at this map, don't forget to fit it to your territory. You're the only one who can confirm the details on the ground. Otherwise, you'll end up like the drunk who lost his keys in the park but is only searching under the streetlight because "that's where the light is." The power of the C.H.A.R.T. framework doesn't come from its literal exactness but from a sense you're moving in the right direction for you.

The following pages are your field guide on the Explorer's Path, but I've also developed online resources specifically designed to complement the book. Below is a link to access self-assessments, video content, and further explorations to help you C.H.A.R.T. your own unique path. These resources are exclusively available to the readers of this book, and I know you'll get value from this extended exploration. Access these resources by heading to www. youendupwhereyoureheading.com/account.

RULES OF THE ROAD

Every good explorer learns the best practices before they set off: don't climb Everest in high winds; red at night, sailors delight; red on yellow, you're a dead fellow; and so on. The Explorer's Path is no different. Heed the rules.

RULE #1: INSPIRATION, NOT ASPIRATION

The stories shared in this book represent the myriad ways to C.H.A.R.T. a path toward a more complete version of yourself. The lives you'll read about aren't meant to be put on pedestals for emulation but are illustrations of how to look at the world differently. Beware if your path starts to look like anyone else's. *Take the spark; don't build the same fire.*

RULE #2: EXPLORE FOR TWO (OR MORE)

You'll require strong, loyal, and trustworthy companions on your adventures. Don't forget to return the favor. Where can you be a mentor? Where can you provide the slightest nudge to help someone get started on their journey? How can you share what you've learned?

RULE #3: YOU MIGHT BE IN THE MIDDLE

Knowing where you're at is just as important as knowing where you're heading. You might not be at the beginning of your journey but in the middle. Identifying your current position can provide peace of mind and a sense of control as you look toward the next step. Keep an eye out for the chapter that feels especially familiar to your current situation.

RULE #4: GET TRACTION

The atomic components of your journey are decisions.

These are the small parts that when stacked together make up the whole. But indecision will stop you in your tracks. At the end of each chapter is a section called "Get Traction." These strategies and questions are designed to help you get a foothold, to gain traction, when the momentum of your journey feels stopped. Action can be useless movement, but traction is progress.

RULE #5: NO SHORTCUTS

You can't skip the hardship. The richest rewards are from personal change, which won't happen if someone carries you across the finish line. There is no "cheat code" or "7 Easy Steps" to become an Explorer, so there's no need to go looking for them.

Final pep talk: You're either exploring your life or you're sitting safely in the settlement waiting for it to be over. It's all within your control. Whenever I'm about to start something hard, I always think about this definition of hell: a meeting you have on your last day on Earth between the person you became and the person you *could* have become.

Your becoming starts now.

PHASE I

CHANGING YOUR MIND

You're at the beginning, but you're acting like it's the end. You've settled. Your daily life is routine and safe but unfulfilling. This place is called your **Charted Territory**, the walls and borders built up around your life.

But something will begin to draw you out. A quiet yearning, a sudden change, or an unsuspecting mentor will open up the edges of your world. These are the **Frontiers** of exploration. The Frontier is the expansiveness of the world you've turned away from or blocked from view—until now.

As you take the first tenuous steps out of your comfort zone, the chorus around you (and inside you) will rise up to hold you back. Movement into the unknown is too scary, too risky, too hard. Yet, the call toward exploration is stronger than the fear. You'll take the first steps toward the discomfort, the excitement, and the challenge drawing you into the new world. This decisive moment is when you **Cross the Bridge**. You've cast off the thought patterns of settling, and the exploration of your life begins.

CHAPTER 1

THE CHARTED TERRITORY

> *"The usual person is more than content, he is even proud, to remain within the indicated bounds, and popular belief gives him every reason to fear so much as the first step into the unexplored."*
>
> —JOSEPH CAMPBELL, *THE HERO WITH A THOUSAND FACES*

"Do you like steak?"

That's the question I would ask, barely waiting for the answer, before spilling out fifty pieces of frozen meat all over someone's living room floor. I wasn't unhinged; I was a door-to-door meat salesman. My post-high school highlight reel was alternating clips of living room meat scatterings and underwhelming community college classes. It wasn't what I'd imagined I'd be doing, but it wasn't terrible. I bought each "case" of meat from the owners of the company and kept the difference from the sale. The more I could sell it for, the more I made. I felt in control.

A good day of sales meant seven to eight hours knocking on doors, and a slow day had me ringing doorbells in the dark. I was getting chased by dogs and yelled off porches, but I rarely took no for an answer. If someone said they didn't have room in their freezer, I'd say, "If I can't get it in, it's free." Five minutes later, they'd have a garbage bag full of old, frozen bread and a freezer full of meat. For the first few months, I felt on top of my little corner of the door-to-door sales world. I was the number one salesman for the company, averaging $150 per sale and could easily make $500–$700 a day. This frozen cash cow provided more money a month than I'd ever had in my life. What more could I ask for?

It turns out, I should have been asking for more. A poorly thought-out "challenge" by one of my bosses showed me how much more. He pulled me aside one morning and said, "Jimmy, if you sell over ten cases today, we'll only charge you $80 per case." Wait, what? I've never claimed to be a math genius, but if I was usually buying them for $105, there's no way they'd take a loss. Each case must have cost less than $80. I was busting my ass making these guys rich while they never got up from their desks. They were functioning in a world well outside the walls I had constructed in my mind.

That afternoon, I Googled the address on the side of one of the meat boxes and tracked down the number of the distributor. Posing as someone who wanted to start a meat company, I called and found out the deal I was getting was worse than I thought; those $105 cases of meat were only $55 wholesale. I was settling and didn't even know it. The next morning, I told my boss about my investigative reporting and gave him an ultimatum: "I'll give you $1,000 to teach me everything I need to know and we can partner or you'll never see me again and you'll make nothing." He leaned back in his swivel chair and surprised me with an even better deal: "Let's partner, and I can get them for $51 a case." That moment changed me forever. The barriers of the settlement had been blown wide open. There wasn't any danger on the other side; there were deals. I never wanted to be on the wrong side of the business equation again. My exploration of entrepreneurship had begun.

So why hadn't I gone into business for myself right away? Why didn't I realize things weren't adding up sooner? Because I was comfortable. I was making more money than I thought a twenty-one-year-old "should." I felt financially safe. The bills were getting paid and then some. My old monkey brain was giving me two thumbs up: we've got enough; stay in line and don't screw it up. That's what kept me (and will keep you) locked into your **Charted Territory**. You keep your face close to the part of your world that's familiar and straightforward because zooming out is scary and unknown. Our brains are designed to make our Charted Territory feel like the *only* territory because it's the safe thing to do—the path of least resistance.

But the lullaby of your Charted Territory is even more devious than keeping you comfortable. You'll justify the safe path because you'll make it feel worth it. It's the narrative you'll spin to match the neurons that have already fired. "I'm working like a dog, but I'm the number one salesman!" This is Maslow's delight theory at work. You maximize the attractions of your current state because questioning them is uncomfortable. But those triumphs are in the service of keeping your feet on the well-trodden paths. Security, predictability, and Netflix to wash it all down at night.

But a moment will come that pulls your head back and reveals the frontiers beyond. It's shocking and scary and sometimes embarrassing you haven't seen them before. You'll want to zoom back in and get comfy; you'll pretend you didn't see it. Campbell calls this pretending the wasteland, "a land of people who are living inauthentic lives. They just get a job because they've got to live and that's rubbish" [1]. But no matter how ordinary your life may seem, you can always turn "waste" into a new way. You have to find the courage to step away from a safe life, to have the life that is waiting for you. I would have been fine making $500 a day selling meat, but I would have missed out on making $5,000 a day as a business owner. You are more than your Charted Territory; you can escape the grind and find new ground.

This first group of Explorers all found themselves in the "wasteland" of their predictable lives. But when the veil lifted on their limited view, they didn't turn away. They stepped beyond the boundaries of the football field, they shook off the limits of their birthplace, and they pushed beyond their labels to seek who they could become.

THE GLASS IS REFILLABLE (DAN CLARK)

The first time I met Dan Clark, I was on a date with one of his neighbors. She knew I loved public speaking and being on stage (I was trying my hand at stand-up comedy at the time) and insisted I meet him. But Dan Clark is not just a speaker; he is *the* speaker. It's like showing up at Tom Brady's house as he's finishing dinner for a quick game of catch. But there I was, at 10:30 p.m. trying to hide my embarrassment as I waited at his door for the "What are you doing at my house?" look. To my relief, he seemed genuinely happy to see us. Dan spent two hours asking me about my life and how he could help. An ordinary day in the life of an Explorer.

Before Dan made it to the Speakers Hall of Fame, everyone thought he was headed for the football hall of fame. He was a projected number one pick for the Oakland Raiders in

1978, a clear and lucrative path in front of him. And then his path fractured, a freak accident in practice leaving him with seven cracked vertebrae in his neck and a severed nerve in his right shoulder. Sixteen doctors around the country told Dan to expect a 10 percent recovery at best. He was told he might not walk again, let alone play football. "It was the loneliest time of my life. All my hopes and dreams were destroyed."

The **Charted Territory** Dan found himself in was filled with sulking and pain. He felt like the road of his life had stopped abruptly, his paralysis extending beyond his body. All the "experts" were pushing him to accept his new way of life, to adjust to the new normal. After more than a year of feeling sorry for himself, a simple question popped into his mind: Why? For months, Dan had been asking: How? How come this happened to me? How can I play football again? How can I get better? Because of his tight grasp to the wrong question, Dan was spinning in place instead of moving forward.

The single question of "why" he wanted to recover was more powerful than any of the "hows" put together. "I thought I was a football player when in reality that's just what I did, it's not who I was. When we identify ourselves in terms of what we do instead of who we are, we become a human 'doing' instead of a human 'being.'" Dan credits his turnaround to a subtle but seismic shift in mindset. He wasn't depressed; he was discouraged. "There's a huge difference between being depressed and being disappointed and being sad. If you spend your life wondering whether your glass is half empty or half full, you've missed the point: it's refillable. Thinking positively doesn't fill up the glass; the pouring does."

Dan started pouring his energy into creating instead of suffering. He worked in the White House for Nancy Reagan's antidrug campaign. He became an international bestselling author, first appearing in the *Chicken Soup for the Soul* series, and wrote chart-topping songs. Dan became a master storyteller, but it didn't come without a little sweat. "I've got a couple of gold records, but I've also written hundreds and hundreds of songs that are so pathetic I wouldn't even share them with my own mother. That's a motivational speech; just keep writing."

Dan took his stories from the page to the stage as he became one of the most-sought-after international speakers. What prepared Dan for speaking wasn't practicing his lines but practicing life:

"As a speaker from the stage, you have to be ordinary before you can be extraordinary. You have these wonderful intros, you know, I have a three-minute introductory video narrated by Larry King that makes me look larger than life and shows video clips of going into space and flying fighter jets and writing gold record songs, but the reality is people don't care if I've ever succeeded, they want to know, 'Clark did you ever fail and fall down?' They don't relate to my perfections, if I even have any, they relate to my imperfections. It's the possibility piece, can I do it too with my weaknesses, with my limitations, and with my strengths, with my history and my past? Every saint has a past and every sinner has a future."

As Dan shares generously with those around him, he knows rewards will come back his way as well. Dan has given over 350 free speeches and donated thousands of hours to different causes. Most of those hours have been in the service of the brave men and women of the United States Armed Forces. In return, he's seen his own dreams come true, having gotten the chance to fly every fighter jet in the Air Force and Navy with two seats (civilians still need some oversight!). "Life is a bank; life is a credit union. Deposit, deposit, deposit so when it comes time for us to withdraw, we have people and resources that come out of the woodwork. People come to me and say, 'You have helped me for so many years, you have served my family, you have served our community, now it's our turn to give back.' The laws of the universe are in place. Karma is a real deal."

THE REFUGEE HUSTLE (HAYSAM SAKAR)

Haysam Sakar may have grown up with a view of the famed pyramids in Egypt, but he always had his sights set on the horizon beyond. "My dad's business was tourism where we had a lot of American, German, and Japanese tourists. I was most intrigued by the American tourists because of their way of thinking, their way of dealing with people. You could feel the freedom of thought, the freedom of expression, and their business mind was extremely open to all possibilities." But Haysam's **Charted Territory** was complicated, creating walls within walls. His father was Palestinian, a refugee driven out of Israel, and his mother was Egyptian. He could never be an Egyptian citizen, and he wasn't born "in the land," so he wasn't considered Palestinian. "I couldn't get an Egyptian ID, I couldn't go to public colleges, public schools, and I couldn't go to any tourist attraction without paying the foreigners fee. We had to pay a yearly visa fee, and if we didn't pay, we would get deported." The barriers and risks of exploring the world beyond seemed insurmountable.

What propelled Haysam forward was an Explorer for a father who showed him walls were meant to be climbed. "Watching him, he always wanted to upgrade, he always wanted to go up. He worked hard, I got that drive from him. I received that information watching him work and watching him hustling." When Desert Storm descended on the Middle East, the family business was no longer viable, and his family lost everything. But to Haysam's father, this was another wall to go over, with delight and growth waiting on the other side. "He drove to a village out in the middle of nowhere and found himself in a 1968 Peugeot wagon. It was literally sitting in a chicken coop, and he took it out and cleaned it, got it running and became a cab driver." Haysam's father refused to settle, and Haysam resolved to follow his lead.

Haysam expanded his own territory with a move to New York City when he was twenty-three years old. He received a small scholarship to a state college but still needed to clear the hurdle of getting a visa. "I walk into the embassy, over 300 people sitting there, everybody wants to go to a country where you can achieve your dreams. I was told in my interview that I would be the only one granted a visa that day." To prove worthy of his selection, Haysam secured a job in NYC only hours after landing. He was tasked with maintenance at a baby formula warehouse, mostly sweeping up dead mice from all of the cats employed to "protect" the product. When the day was done, Haysam gratefully fell asleep in his windowless four-by-six corrugated steel room without windows. He knew those walls wouldn't keep him in for long.

Over the next decade, Haysam explored the ins and outs of any business he came across. He waited tables in Times Square, he did AC and refrigeration repair, he drove a limo and delivery trunks, and he did demolition for home remodels for which he still has the scars. "You put in the effort, you hustle, you talk to people, and you shine above the next guy, you get the next promotion, you do whatever needs to be done. I knew it would be hard. I didn't know it would be this hard, but I was ready. I had two choices. Make it or die." For Haysam, settling did not feel safer.

By the time he was thirty-five, the limited territory of the unwanted refugee who landed in the US with thirty-seven dollars in his pocket had been transformed into the triumph of a successful entrepreneur who finally had a place to call home and the citizenship to prove it. Like his father before him, he had gone to the middle of nowhere and provided for his family, building two successful car dealerships from the ground up. Haysam knows he's built more than a used car lot, he's built trust. "It's not a car sale and it's over. You take care of the customer, you don't make all your money on one guy. A lot of people here think you make all your money on one deal. Don't be short-term greedy; be long-term greedy. Don't make it all on one person and show them that, and you'll gain loyalty." As an entrepreneur, Haysam measures himself by an old Egyptian tale. "In Egypt, in the time of the Pharaohs, when you go to the gates you're asked two questions when waking up from the dead: Have you found joy in life, and have you brought joy to others' lives? This is how you are judged. How much joy have you received? How much joy have you given? That, to me, is one of the most profound things, as simple as it is, to find joy and give joy. There can be stressful times in life, but that's life. You have to focus on finding joy, receiving and giving."

DRUMMING UP POSITIVITY (CLINT PULVER)

When Clint Pulver was a kid, he couldn't sit still. He tapped, drummed, wiggled, and annoyed everyone at his elementary school. "The Twitcher," as he was not lovingly nicknamed, spent more time in the hallway than he did in class. "I had to move. I would move through tapping, playing with pencils, hitting the desk, tapping my feet, and obviously if you've ever sat next to someone who's clicking their pen or they're tapping their foot, it gets annoying fast." Clint's world was movement when everyone else wanted him to settle down.

After an epic session of tapping in Mr. Jensen's class, an older teacher with Coke bottle glasses, Clint was asked to stay after. Clint figured this was the final straw—he was about to get kicked out of school for good. Mr. Jensen pulled up a big chair, and Clint slid down in a little one. He said, "Listen, I want you to know you're not in trouble. Try this. Can you tap your head and rub your belly at the same time?" Clint gave it a go, and he could do it. "Now switch. Now rub your head and tap your belly." Clint easily switched, surprising even himself. Mr. Jensen laughed, sat back in his chair, and said, "I don't think you're a problem. I think you're a drummer." And with those words, Clint's days as a hopeless troublemaker were behind him. Mr. Jensen saw something in Clint he hadn't seen in himself. He cleared away the restrictions of Clint's **Charted Territory** and let him tap (quite literally) into his unmet potential. As Clint got up to leave, Mr. Jensen pulled out a pair of drumsticks, put them in Clint's hands, and said, "These are for you, but you have to promise you'll keep them in your hands as much as you can. Keep them in your hands, and let's see what happens."

Twenty-one years later, Clint did his best to keep his promise. He toured all over the world with his drumsticks, even making a stop on the TV show *America's Got Talent*. He graduated from college in 2012 with zero debt because of music scholarships and paying gigs. "Because of one person, one person who believed in me, one person who saw a problem as an opportunity. He saw the problem as the solution, and in doing so, I lived a better life. He wrote a better story for me." It's easy to be a critic, to figure out what's wrong with a business or your spouse or your neighbor, but as Clint says, "The miracles happen when you figure out what's right. When you change that lens, when you change that perception, you alter your reality."

After college, Clint "chased the money" and went into medical sales but knew it wasn't what he was meant to do. He had slipped back into the confines of a limited Charted Territory and, out of desperation, put out an idea to a group of friends. "Guys, wouldn't it be crazy if you could find one job, one career, that allowed you to do what you love most of the time, that provided financially for your needs and contributed to your purpose in life?" His friends laughed;

that kind of life was an anomaly. Clint agreed. He wanted to be an anomaly again. Two weeks later, he quit his job and jumped headfirst into the world of professional speaking. "The day I quit my job was the day I can say that I started living. One of the best decisions I ever made." As a young speaker, Clint thought he'd connect best with middle and high school students. He felt these would be the warm-up crowds before working with more expensive clients. "With 3,000 kids surrounding you, it's the toughest arenas you can speak at." Despite the challenge, Clint was a hit with schools and caught the eye of corporations looking to connect with their younger employees.

Clint quickly realized he was dealing with an era of management who wanted their employees to sit still and settle instead of looking for "drummers." But the command-and-control managers he was coaching would need more than his anecdote about Mr. Jensen to change their organizations; they'd need data. He stumbled upon the idea of going undercover after meeting with the CEO of a large sporting goods store. Although the CEO was open to adapting his business to keep pace with market changes, he wanted his management style to stay the same. He told Clint, "The way I manage today is the same way I managed twenty years ago." When the meeting ended, Clint wandered the store in his backward hat and tracksuit and casually talked with the mostly millennial or Gen Z employees. "I asked them questions like, 'What's it like to work here?' 'Do you see yourself working here long term?' 'Do you feel like you're listened to?' I interviewed six employees, and five out of the six said they wouldn't be working for him in his store in three months or less." Clint was getting the raw, unedited feedback the CEO didn't know he needed.

Clint's guerrilla data collection became the basis for Undercover Speaker, a global program with lasting impact for his corporate clients. Clint's penchant for movement, for exploring, was unearthing the truth needed for change. "They thought I was literally someone off the street coming in to see what it's like to work there. What I got was the closest thing to the truth you could get. It wasn't some survey. A lot of companies do surveys. But I remember when I was in Corporate America and the uppers gave us a survey, I never answered honestly." When Clint presents to executive teams and national conferences, the authentic data creates a real drive to push beyond the Charted Territory of decades-old management practices. Clint beams when he talks about the changes he sees when following up with his clients. "It increases retention; you get higher engagement and better loyalty. It's different, it's unique, and I love it."

As a professional speaker, Clint has achieved the anomalous life he was after. He loves what he does, it provides for him financially, and his work has purpose. But he never forgets who helped get him there. When Clint goes undercover, he's looking to pay back his debt to Mr. Jensen. He's helping companies become advocates for their employees, to search below the problem and find the potential. Clint knows firsthand when you "act like a Mr. Jensen, we never forget you."

WELCOME TO YOUR FIRST *TRAIL MARKER!*

These callouts are here to highlight the "who's who" of archetypes you're likely to encounter on your journey. The people you invite on your explorations will greatly impact where you end up and who you'll be when you get there. Companions can speed you up (for better or worse) or slow you down (for better or worse). They can make the adventure a pleasure or keep you focused on the pain. The decision of who to surround yourself with is critical and shouldn't be done passively. Don't settle; be selective.

TRAIL MARKER #1

FIND A GUIDE WHO LIKES DOUGHNUTS

Exploration without guidance is an unnecessary risk. You need people who can give you feedback on your planned path, help you get started or unstuck, and steer you away from the common mistakes so you can go make the uncommon ones. The Hero's Journey calls these figures **Mentors**, but I'll refer to them as **Guides**. These are the Explorers who have gone before you and returned from their journey to advise the next round of seekers.

Some people believe having a Guide is "cheating"; they want a bootstrap story, a solo act. And although the lone explorer may be a romantic tale, it's a dishonest one. No one makes it on their own. As Maslow put it, our Guides allow us to "feel safe and beckon us onward to try the new experience." Invest in the success of your explorations by securing and putting your trust in experienced Guides.

Clint's story is the perfect example of how different figures in our lives can look at the same attribute (fidgeting) and come to completely different conclusions of its value (detrimental or beneficial). A great Guide like Mr.

Jensen doesn't pick up a doughnut and see the hole; he sees a delicious doughnut. He's not focused on what's missing ("This pastry has a huge hole in the middle of it—huge mistake!"); he's on the lookout for what's there ("This pastry is shaped like a ring—what a differentiator!"). He beckoned Clint forward to try on a new identity as a drummer and as an Explorer of his unique talents.

I experienced a "doughnut" moment myself when I was on a mission in Mexico (more on this in chapter 4). Not long after my arrival, I got the reputation of being a "little bit out there" and "too loud" for the work we were doing. To be fair, we were supposed to conduct ourselves with "quiet dignity," but I figured it didn't apply to people like me. I worked with high energy and entertainment and couldn't easily tone it down. After a few weeks, one of the more serious missionaries complained to our mission president that I was being disruptive and my actions weren't "close enough to the spirit." Everyone around me thought my approach had a hole.

In our next one-to-one meeting, I was sure the president was going to give me the "take it down a notch" lecture. Instead, he saw the doughnut. Although he thought being reverent might work for some of the other missionaries, he recognized it wasn't right for me. "Elder Rex, this is going to be the most important thing I tell you on your mission. Don't change. Don't ever change who you are—not for me, not for other missionaries, or anyone else. You have a gift, and God made you this way because you open hearts and doors nobody else ever could. So don't worry about the others; I see you. I wish I had 200 missionaries just like you." He empowered me to embrace all of my strengths and not worry about being anything but myself.

So when it comes time to search out a Guide, look for someone who will help you harness who you are instead of being hell-bent on "fixing" who you aren't. The Mr. Jensens of the world will see the untapped potential hidden in every quirk.

WINDOW OF OPPORTUNITY (SUSAN PETERSEN)

Susan Petersen had an unsuccessful Etsy shop and an equally unsuccessful blog. So when she posted about the leather moccasins she'd made for her newborn son, she expected more yawns. To her surprise, people went nuts. She hadn't planned on making them to sell, but Susan quickly went through all the scrap leather she had on hand to meet the interest. She naively thought you could buy a few clippings of leather but found out you needed to "buy the whole cow, legs, belly, and all." The $200 price tag was $200 more than she could spare as her **Charted Territory** was food stamps and barely getting by.

The easy path would have been a return to basic survival, but Susan wanted to thrive. Instead of settling for brief success, she spent the next month banging on windows (quite literally) to raise money for her materials. Her brother had a window installation business, and he would remove and haul away the old windows encased in aluminum. Instead of trash, Susan saw dollar signs. When her kids were asleep, Susan would bang the glass out of the windows and stack the aluminum. "I would chain them up so no one could steal them. At the end of a couple of months, I took all the frames to the scrap yard and got $200."

The hustle didn't stop at windows; Susan wanted doors opened as well. At a blogging conference, she saw the opportunity to achieve one of her goals: to get on the TV show *Shark Tank*. She recognized a former entrepreneur from the show and laid on the charm. Three weeks later, she was filming and pitching a stake in her company, Freshly

Picked. The sharks loved Susan's story, but one by one, they declined to invest. In the end, it was down to offers from only Kevin and Damon. Considering the fate of her company, Susan recalls thinking, "I love Kevin, but I thought Damon made a lot of sense from a consumer goods point of view." With a handshake from Damon, Susan had gone from food stamps to venture funding.

After the show, the dream deal fell apart, and Susan was back to being a solo act. Susan was too used to doing things her own way and couldn't get on the same page with Damon. "I think a trap entrepreneurs fall into is, you think one investor or one employee is going to change your business, and it's totally false. It's getting up every day, working on your business, and putting in the time to make sure you're in a good spot." Susan's appearance on the show, regardless of a deal, had put her in a good spot. Demand was booming.

The next phase of the business was not something Susan was ready to handle on her own. Shortly after *Shark Tank*, with a new manufacturer secured, she had a 25 percent off sale to celebrate. She ended up with 2,000 orders she couldn't deliver on. "I went home and cried. I was shocked all day. I looked at it as the worst thing ever because I had people's money and nothing to give them." Susan reached out to a friend for advice and got the harsh wake-up call she needed. "Okay. Are you done crying? Boo-F'ing-Hoo, Susan. It's so hard to be successful." When Susan said she was going to return everyone's money, her friend turned up the pressure. "No, you're not. I'm going to tell you what you're going to do. You're going to go to bed. You're going to get up tomorrow morning. You're going to put on your big girl panties, and you're going to take care of this, and you're going to get it done." This Guide had teeth. Susan reached out to every customer and told them to expect a delay. No one canceled.

Four years into her business, Susan is continually looking for new Guides to challenge her. When she reaches a new phase in the business, she finds someone who's been there before and unleashes the questions. "I'm very bold when I meet people. I never want people to feel like I'm using them, so I'm up front about what's happening. I don't learn much from business books. I think there's a lot of truth in there, but I learn more from talking to people and understanding."

EXPAND THE BORDERS OF YOUR WORLD

Your **Charted Territory** feels like everything until it isn't. The moment will come when the singular path outlined by your family, your culture, or even your own fear opens up to a multitude of possibilities. The path of the Explorer is boundless, regardless of the walls that seem to be keeping you in. Once you've seen the new paths of your potential, it'll be impossible to stay put.

GET TRACTION

1. **You're a human being, not a human doing.** You are not your profession or your hobby or your label. As Dan Clark found out, when you let what you do define who you are, two things happen: you limit your territory to the borders of your "doing," and you turn your self-worth over to something which can change in an instant. When Dan switched his focus to being, to exploring, he found himself in a limitless territory and in charge of his own value.

2. **Identify your walls so you can climb over them.** The limits of your Charted Territory can give you an excuse not to grow, but it doesn't mean growth isn't possible. Haysam Sakar took the limited identity of a poor refugee and transformed himself into a successful business owner. He knew no one would fault him for staying behind the wall, but he wouldn't forgive himself if he didn't try to climb over it. Where are your walls? How are you being held back under the guise of safety or low expectations? What makes you say, "I can't because..." or "I would but..."? Those are the artificial barriers you need to push yourself over.

3. **Turn your "problems" into potential.** One of the confines you might encounter is a perceived "unfixable" personal trait. You're too shy or too disorganized or too short to be an Explorer so you'll settle for something else. Clint Pulver would say you need to figure out how to turn that attribute into an asset. If what you have to offer isn't working in your Charted Territory, you probably need a change of scenery.

4. **Look through a different window.** If you want to break free of your Charted Territory, perspective is everything. Is a stack of old windows junk or startup capital? Susan Petersen refused to look at her situation as hopeless and instead saw a world of possibility right in her own backyard.

Settlers complain about their circumstances, Explorers get creative.

You found your way outside the settlement, nothing but open space in front of you. What looked like the end is now the beginning. But which way should you go? If you want to end somewhere different, you need to start somewhere different. Welcome to the **Frontier**.

CHAPTER 2

FACING THE FRONTIER

"*Destiny has summoned the hero and transferred his spiritual center of gravity from within the pale of his society to a zone unknown.*"

—JOSEPH CAMPBELL, *THE HERO WITH A THOUSAND FACES*

"There are 6 million children in modern day slavery. Most of them in sex trafficking." When I heard those words, it felt like a ton of bricks had been dropped on my chest. The man who spoke them, Paul Hutchinson, was raising money and awareness for an organization called Operation Underground Railroad (OUR), a nonprofit on a mission to end child slavery worldwide. As Paul spoke about his personal involvement in rescuing children and those still enslaved, a new part of the world (a horrific part to be sure) was opened to me. I saw a path ahead of me where I couldn't only be a real estate agent; I had to be a change agent like Paul.

I've never felt stronger about a direction in my life as I did that day.

I went up to Paul after the event and said, "I'm in. I want to help." He nodded, smiled, and directed me to the website, no doubt having heard people utter those sincere words with no action to follow them. But I wasn't there for lip service. "You don't understand. I want in." He informed me I was the one who didn't understand. There were over 300 people in line to go on a rescue operation and most of them were former Navy SEALS. Navy SEALS? I was a former door-to-door meat salesman; no wasn't in my vocabulary. "You're an idiot sales guy like me and you get to do this. Tell me how." He realized I wasn't going away and made me put my money where my mouth was: a $5,000 table at an event the next week. "Put me down for one."

When I showed up and paid for the table, Paul took me seriously for the first time. He invited me to lunch and explained how the operations worked and how I could be part of a team. The part available to me was the goofy side-kick to the undercover Special Forces. Imagine the part in a movie where the leader of a heist team turns to the dumb sidekick and says, "Okay, so while we're waiting safely on the sidelines, your job is to be the bait." But this wasn't a movie and the danger I'd be putting myself in was real.

Me: "Got it, the bait. What else?"

Paul: "Well, you're going to have to pay."

The number he told me was the same price tag as my new truck. Paul laughed as I wrote a check and slid it across the table.

Me: "What else?"

Paul: "You've gotta get trained. Call Jackson."

Jackson was a master at Krav Maga, a self-defense and fighting system developed in the 1950s for the Israeli Army. It's used by the FBI, SWAT teams, and real estate agents who volunteer to be the bait for bad guys. This was the Guide who was going to teach me how to fight to kill, and I hoped like hell I'd never have to do it. The opening pages of this book (Path Two) were a loose reenactment of my first mission. The bad guys went down without me directly involved in the fight, but I had been standing inside the arena. My territory was now international humanitarian, and I'd never go back to the sidelines.

A new **Frontier** can present itself in many ways. It could be a subtle yearning, "ripples on the surface of life, produced by unsuspected springs" [1], or a bright, neon sign that can't be turned off (like my experience with Paul). A Frontier could come upon you by accident: a chance meeting or passage in a book that strikes at your core. Whatever the case, you'll know when you've seen a new path, and it will be impossible to see the world the same again. Once I heard what was happening to those kids with my own ears, I couldn't unhear it. Even if I had known about the danger I would face, it wouldn't have stopped me. Campbell describes this as "outgrowing the familiar life horizon" where your old way of doing things in the world no longer fits with where you now stand. [2]

You've probably seen new Frontiers in your life and ignored most of them. That doesn't mean you're not an Explorer; it means you're human. When an untraveled path shows up, fear and comfort also make appearances to stop you in your tracks. It's the one-two punch of survival that's worked for thousands of years: seek known pleasure and avoid pain. Just *thinking* about something unpleasant can induce physiological feelings of pain. So it's not surprising when I see people blindly following the path of least resistance and closing themselves off to new experiences. You swipe away the news story instead of doing something about it.

But you can teach an old brain new tricks. When you venture into the unknown, you'll find the discomfort to be temporary. When you forge new Frontiers, you'll uncover pleasure in places that seemed devoid of it. Yet, overcoming your fear is only half the battle. You've got to deal with everyone else as well. When I told my friends and family about going on OUR missions, they told me

I was crazy. My girlfriend at the time pleaded with me not to go; she couldn't see why I was taking this unnecessary risk and finally said, "Why can't they go and do it?" Without thinking I responded, "We *are* the 'they.'" Those words sent chills down my spine because I knew how true they were in the core of my being. It's a mindset I carry with me to this day. There is no "they" when it comes to your own life. The writer and podcaster Johnathan Fields calls what my ex-girlfriend was doing "superimposing limitations":

> "The well-intended pronouncement by others, often those we trust, that something that calls us isn't worthy of our continued love, energy, and attention because it doesn't fit the mold of what they deem a valid or worthy use of time. They can't see how it'd lead to success were they to try it, so they assume it couldn't lead to success for anyone else, and deem its pursuit invalid or, worse, irresponsible." [3]

Your loved ones and friends will project their own discomfort and value systems onto your actions. This is a "transferred limitation" and should be carefully guarded against. Your own fear is enough to overcome; don't take on everyone else's. The following Explorers are examples of what it looks like to push past fear and discomfort. They are unique, but they share the common ground of stepping forward toward an unknown terrain, moving purposefully into the Frontier.

WHEN BATMAN WON'T PICK UP THE PHONE (TIM BALLARD)

Tim Ballard started his career at the CIA and later went to Homeland Security after 9/11. He was thrown into the front lines of a developing unit working on child crimes and trafficking. "The deeper I got, the more shocked I became. I never stopped being shocked." Tim didn't know he was living in a world where an estimated 6 million kids are slaves (slave labor, organ harvesting, and sex trafficking). "With the amount of money made in human trafficking today, you could buy every Starbucks in the world, every NBA team, and still have enough money left over to send every American kid to college for four years."

Despite the staggering and sickening facts urging him to push for change, Tim felt stifled by the restrictions of international jurisdiction. As an undercover operative, Tim could see the full scope of the problem they were dealing with but was stopped short of taking action. "The problem moved so fast. You'd find one trafficking victim here, but there were five countries that kid might have been through." As a US agent, Tim was not authorized to rescue children if the case wasn't connected to the US or couldn't be tried in the US. His frustration was mounting. "I thought if there was a private organization that worked legally, ethically, and under the right jurisdiction, we could get things done. We needed a glorified informant who could move quicker and support what needed to be done." But Tim's informant didn't exist, and his hands were tied. "So many times, I thought, man, if I could pick up the phone, like the Batman phone, and say, 'Hey, Batman, can you go do something for me? Because I can't get over there; it's outside my jurisdiction.'"

After years of standing by and watching traffickers slip through his fingers, Tim felt the pull to forge this new **Frontier** himself. The pivotal moment came after meeting with a Haitian man whose three-year-old son had been kidnapped by traffickers. "I went to my wife and said, 'I promised this man I'd help him find his son; no one's helping him, and I don't have enough money to do it on my own.'" Tim's wife knew he needed a push into this new Frontier. "My wife was so brave. She said, 'You have no choice. You've been called to do this. You know it's the right thing to do.' And there's a sense of comfort there because all it would take in that moment is for her to say, 'You're right. I'm scared,' and I would not have done it" [4]. Tim made the leap and quit his job, founding Operation Underground Railroad (O.U.R.) in December 2013.

Tim raised enough money for one or two operations before his life savings would be exhausted. "It's a scary thing to leave a comfortable job and start a nonprofit—a nonprofit that wants to do something most people are saying you can't do." One of the first missions Tim planned was to Haiti to seek out the little boy he had promised to find. The team was successful in finding the person who captured the boy, and they liberated twenty-eight kids from sexual exploitation. But heart wrenchingly, none of those kids was the one Tim was looking for; he had been sold to another trafficker before the mission. Despite the relative success, Tim felt like a failure. But the father of the boy pulled Tim aside to embolden him. "It's okay that my son wasn't found. You guys wouldn't have come here were it not for my son. If I have to give up my son so these twenty-eight kids can be rescued, that's a burden I'm willing to bear."

Tim has received an outpouring of support that has sustained his cause. From small online donations to support from the radio host Glenn Beck and millions of dollars in backing from Tony Robbins, Tim's story is spurring action and results. Although official numbers can't be released to ensure continued government cooperation, OUR estimates that they've helped liberate thousands of kids from slavery and put away over 400 sex traffickers. While these are incredible figures, Tim's reward comes from a number that's hard to count. "One trafficker will sexually abuse up to a hundred kids in a lifetime. So if we put away eighteen guys, that's probably close to eighteen hundred kids who will never know they needed rescuing. Those are the rescues I love to think about."

Today, the hardest part for Tim is fighting the urge to stay on the front lines. "When we first started, it was me and one part-time guy. I did mostly operations in the first couple of years, and then we got big enough that my wife had to lead an intervention. She said, 'Listen, we can afford to hire people to do this now. When you go on an op, our donations go down.'" The wise Guide had spoken again, and Tim knew it was time to start a new chapter for O.U.R. "My role had changed. I needed to be the guy doing interviews, converting people to the cause, and making sure the guys on the ground have what they need."

Tim's new mission is to educate the world about the seriousness and scope of child trafficking today. The story of O.U.R.'s founding will hit the big screen in 2020 with the theatrical release of *Sound of Freedom* starring Jim Caviezel as Tim. "We read history books about when slavery existed and we all say to ourselves, I would have been an abolitionist. I would not have stood by and done nothing. Then I say to them, you have that chance now. If you would have done something then, then do something right now. There are more people in slavery today than ever before in the history of the world. Here's your chance. Are you going to stand up or not?"

TRAIL MARKER #2

GIVE TO BE GUIDED

People often ask me how they can be more successful in their lives or businesses. I tell them to find someone with experience and put in the hard work to earn their trust. But Guides aren't waiting around to help you out; they're exploring like you. To help unlock the breadth of their wisdom, you have to align with their goals.

The check that I wrote Paul Hutchinson to fund an O.U.R. operation wasn't what sealed the deal on my involvement; it was because I kept my word. He'd had hundreds of people write checks and express an interest in going on a mission, but almost no one followed through. Some people wrote the check, fewer took the training, and even fewer were available when it was time to go. After our first mission together, Paul told me, "The reason I chose you is because you did everything you said you were going to do. I knew I could count on you. That's so rare in this world. I help run a 17 billion-dollar fund, I make valuations every day, but you can't put a value on someone you can always count on."

In the end, my investment of time to show up for Paul earned the trust of an incredible Guide. He shared his passion, his wisdom, and a network of incredible people. An Explorer is always lifted beyond their limited reach by the Guides they seek to serve.

RIDE THE WAVE (TREVOR MILTON)

Seeing a new **Frontier** that others ignore is Trevor Milton's specialty. He started a multimillion-dollar video surveillance company at age twenty-two. He beat eBay and Amazon to the punch with the nationwide online classified website upillar.com that had 60 million views the first day it went live. And just to switch things up, he established dHybrid Systems, a compressed natural gas fuel system manufacturer that sold to Worthington Industries in 2014 for a reported $16 million. But as a serial entrepreneur, Trevor's main goal is to learn. "I was building multiple companies trying to learn the hard lessons that every entrepreneur has to learn."

Trevor's most influential teacher was the heavy-duty trucking industry. Before they pivoted toward fuel systems, dHybrid was focused on diesel engines. "We would take these big diesel engines, recalibrate them, and try to fix them so they would run cleaner, less emissions, and more efficient." But calibration could only go so far, and Trevor felt "how quickly this zero-emission world was coming at us." The vast Frontier of clean energy was pulling Trevor in.

With the green energy tidal wave building in the distance, Trevor knew he had to enter this new world decisively or risk getting stuck behind the competitors to come. "I either had to jump in or not, ride the wave or not, because if you're behind it, you can't ride the momentum. Entrepreneurship was already hard enough, so being behind the wave wasn't an option. If you're focusing on something that's not working easily, it's probably the wrong thing to focus on. Businesses are like a current in the river. The easiest path is going to be the most successful path. If you're fighting the current, you're in the wrong industry."

Trevor paddled into a new current at full speed toward his most audacious endeavor yet: Nikola Motors, a company focused on electric heavy-duty applications. While Elon Musk's Tesla was zeroed in on daily commutes and short-haul trucking, Trevor and team found their wave with long-haul technology and infrastructure. "We were in the perfect position, we got ahead of it, we built this zero-emission electric semitruck with hydrogen on it. It can outperform diesel in every category." Not content to rush their truck to production with existing components, Nikola built their semi from the ground up. Trevor beams when he talks about what his team had created. "It's like this bullet train. It looks beautiful; it's all electric and it's silent. There's no emissions, and it'll go zero to sixty faster than most cars. It's amazing. It's probably the most successful private launch of a product in American history."

The Nikola One racked up $6 billion in presales, and the most recent round of funding valued the upstart company at over $3 billion. Trevor was out front and being propelled by the current, but designing and selling the truck turned out to be the easy part. "The hard thing now that you have all these orders is how do you fulfill them? How do you make sure the truck is totally fit for production? How do you make sure that it's not going to break down and there are no issues with safety and reliability? That's the hard stuff, but those are things you can hire people to figure out."

With the vision created and sold, strong Allies were drawn to Nikola. The people Trevor hired to "figure things out" were all leaders in their field. "We've got world-class people who were running 10 to 15 billion-dollar companies and they're coming to work for us now." Trevor knows that the CEOs and company presidents wouldn't be swayed by money or a title; they already had every opportunity they could want. "They'll only jump on board if they feel inspired, if they feel like it's going to change their lives and change the world. They can see the current."

Having learned the hard lessons in previous companies, Trevor understood his early hires would make or break Nikola. "It's almost impossible for you to be successful if you have people in your life who are creating chaos or dragging you down emotionally. It's critically important to surround yourself with people that give as much as you do." Trevor uses the story of Fred Smith, the founder of FedEx, as a reason to keep his foot pressed firmly on the gas (or electric pedal in this case). "He almost lost his entire company because of the oil embargo. There's no reason why America can't completely depend on itself. We're the only trucking manufacturer in the world that builds our own truck and provides our own fuel. When you buy your truck from us, you get unlimited fuel and it's all done right here in America. World War III and IV can break out and it wouldn't affect our business plan." Trevor Milton is out in front.

FAILURE ISN'T AN OPTION (JANE ANN CRAIG)

Jane Ann Craig was sitting next to the hospital bed where her husband had just passed away. She felt an overwhelming grief, coupled with a strong need to survive and thrive for her two-year-old son. When her own father died, Jane Ann didn't handle it well, but she vowed to step up this time and wasn't going to let her son "lose both parents that night." Jane Ann made a promise to herself and to her son that every choice thereafter would be to ensure him a full and happy childhood. When she crossed the threshold of that hospital room as a single parent, she was still grieving but more determined than ever.

Jane Ann needed to go all in for her son to have the life that she envisioned for him. So when the insurance company she worked for wanted to expand her sales territory and have her travel more, she had to draw the line. "I realized that this vehicle called my job of sixteen years no longer supported my goals and dreams, so I made the decision to quit. It was a sudden decision." In order to have the flexibility she needed, Jane Ann needed to be her own boss. She would have to start her own company. Before she could change her mind, Jane Ann typed up her resignation letter and immediately drove it to Kinko's to send it overnight. Weeks later, she was sitting on her floor saying, "Oh my god. What did I do?" She had crossed into the **Frontier** of self-employment, and there was no turning back.

From the outside looking in, the risk Jane Ann was taking seemed massive. She'd never had an executive management position, she'd never built a company from scratch, and she'd never raised capital. She didn't qualify for a loan, she didn't have any money, and she hadn't even taken a basic accounting class. What Jane Anne did have was drive and fire in excess. She sought out a Guide, her brother and a CPA, and together they built a business plan and financial projections to create her own insurance company. "Insurance is highly regulated. It's considered a financial industry. It was not my first choice. But I'd been a receptionist and I'd served in some other roles. So I knew insurance better than anything else. I needed to provide and be there for my son, and creating my own insurance company was the vehicle to do that."

With a strong purpose (and now a plan), Jane Ann pitched everyone she knew on her business to raise capital. They all said no—even her family. It wasn't until a conversation with a former business partner of her father's that she realized her approach was wrong. She was selling the plan, not the purpose. Jane Ann needed Allies who believed in her, not projections on a spreadsheet. She stopped pitching and started predicting her future. When someone asked her what she was up to, she'd say, "I'm building a business, and it's going to be a vehicle to help us achieve our goals, dreams, and visions. Not only is it going to be a great investment, it's going to create hundreds of jobs and we're going to be able to support causes that we're passionate about." Suddenly, people were interested.

With funding secured, Jane Ann turned to building her team. She couldn't afford established players in the field, so youth and passion drove her hiring. "My team was young. If you interview them now, they'd say, 'I couldn't believe that you hired me and that you treated me like an adult.' I totally relied on them; they were creative, they had a lot to prove, and I was able to train them and mentor them." Jane Ann's team supplied the energy, and she provided the vision without constraints. The naivete of the team and what they could accomplish turned out to be the company's greatest strength. When Jane Ann recently reconnected with one of her first employees, she recalled one of the defining moments of her career when Jane Ann asked her for the sales number for the month. The answer turned out to be thirty-eight, more sales than any Jane Ann had seen in her entire career, and she told her how remarkable it was. "That struck me because you had never set a limit on us. We didn't know. I didn't know that was good."

Jane Ann's team continued to exceed expectations, and she made good on the promise to her initial investors and, more importantly, her son. She sold her multimillion-dollar companies to BlueCross BlueShield for a substantial profit. With plenty on the line in a highly regulated business, Jane Ann never wavered. "Failure wasn't an option for me. I didn't allow myself to get fearful. I had shareholders and employees, and I was accountable to them. And when things got really, really rough, which they do when you're building a business, I would think about my son."

With a new chapter as a consultant and author, Jane Ann is sharing her story for new entrepreneurs venturing into their own Frontiers. In her first book, *The Audit Principle: 5 Powerful Steps to Align Your Life with the Laws of Success*, she details how she brought purpose and strategy into her life and business. It was the book Jane Anne wished she had at the beginning of her own journey. To bring things full circle, she asked the main character in her book, her son, to write the foreword. It took only one line for Jane Ann to know that it had all been worth it. It read, "My mom became extraordinary so she could do something ordinary, which is to be my mom, which I think is extraordinary."

TRAIL MARKER #3

DON'T HIDE THE HARDSHIP FROM YOUR ALLIES

A truly worthwhile adventure is more than you can accomplish on your own. The people who stand by your side, calm you down, and lift you up are your **Allies**. An Ally can be a business partner, a friend, a spouse, or an employee. An Ally is someone who shares your purpose and stretches out an arm when you're dangling from the cliff. You attract and retain a strong supporting cast by drawing them into your vision of the world.

A wise Guide of mine once said, "Jimmy, I don't ever want you to look at what's coming out of the funnel; only focus on what you put into it. Relationships, work, your time and efforts, everything. You can control what goes in, but you can't control what comes out." You're in control of what you bring on your journey, and that especially applies to Allies. Are your current friends and coworkers the type of people you always dreamed about sharing a life with? Or do you have partnerships and friendships by proximity? Not to say that your best friend from fifth grade can't be a good Ally, but it's more than likely that a wider net will produce a stronger Ally. Your adventures will require more than accidental Allies. Build your team with intention.

You are going to be afraid to open up to those around you about your struggles and fears because you believe it will make you look weak. You'll tell a dishonest story and your Allies will support it and won't offer the help you desperately need. The inspiration for Jane Ann's book, *The Audit Principle*, came from her initial inability to tell an honest story about a routine audit of her business. As she dug into the books, she found they were badly out of compliance in several areas. And instead of immediately rallying her team, she told a weak story. She pretended the problems weren't there; she made excuses and even tried to find someone to blame. But she realized those approaches weren't relevant; they were "time thieves." When she went to her team for help, to normalize a process of finding and celebrating mistakes, stress around audits became a thing of the past.

I told my own dishonest story when I was trying to claw out of debt after the 2008 market collapse. I was personally and professionally drowning. I was calling hundreds of For Sale by Owners per week but had little to show for it. I still had sales coming in, more than most agents at the time, but they weren't coming from the strategies I was working on with my real estate coach Bill Pipes. On our weekly calls, I exaggerated about how things were going, not wanting him to think I was failing at what he was teaching, so he kept encouraging me to stay the course.

But I hated the course. At the end of 2009, I quit real estate for three months to clear my head. I became a high school baseball coach and went back to finish my bachelor's degree. Anything but real estate. At the beginning of 2010, I decided to give it one more shot, but honestly this time. At our annual planning meeting, I came clean to Bill about where my sales were coming from and how unhappy I was doing For Sale by Owners. Instead of berating me, he said, "Well, why didn't you say so? Jimmy, let's design your dream life and build your business around it." My dream life was going to parties with my friends, traveling the world, and giving to charities. I couldn't see how selling real estate fit into that.

But armed with my true story, my Ally and Guide could finally help me. Bill completely reversed my approach to business and changed my life in the process. I went from being a pursuer, chasing For Sale by Owners which I hated, to an attractor. Bill said, "If you want to get everything you want in life, help other people get what they want." I started spoiling my friends (and future clients) with lavish parties and volunteering with different charitable organizations. I traveled the world with anyone who asked, making lasting connections that would end up more than paying for the airfare. Bill's advice sparked the framework that would become The Social Realtor, my real estate coaching business. I stopped hiding and got the help I needed to start living.

Only when you're honest about your struggle can your Allies rise to the occasion and help lift you up.

"There is only one thing worse than fighting with allies, and that is fighting without them."

—WINSTON CHURCHILL

BE OPEN TO THE EDGES

Had I not been at that networking event where Paul spoke about O.U.R., I would've missed a new Frontier that changed the direction of my life. I wouldn't have gone on eleven operations where I personally saw the rescue of over a hundred children and the arrest of more than forty sex traffickers. That Frontier did not exist on my daily commute or show up in my inbox. I had to push at the edges of my Charted Territory and be open when something wanted to pull me in.

GET TRACTION

1. **Find your Why.** Without a big enough "why," a new Frontier is only fear. You'll zero in on the risk and won't be able to see the reward beyond. It's the "Why do I want to do this?" not the "What do I want to accomplish?" that will push you through the inevitable hardship you'll encounter. Is there a wrong in the world that you wish you could help set right like Tim Ballard? Is there a business opportunity you can't believe is being neglected like Trevor Milton? Is there someone in your life who needs you to show up like Jane Ann Craig? Curiosity and necessity will light the way to your why.

2. **Make the Trade.** If you don't have to give something up to forge into your new Frontier, it's not a calling, it's a hobby (which is fine if you want to stay put). Tim and Jane Ann gave up the security of a full-time job. Trevor put his money and reputation on the line. You might start small in what you're giving up (weekend leisure hours to focus on your blog) but the trade-off should feel real; it shouldn't be easy.

3. **Find a Guide.** Take the time to find the experts in your field so they can help you avoid the common mistakes. You'll make plenty of uncommon ones, so save yourself the time.

4. **Give Yourself Permission to Explore Without the Baggage.** Shooting for a $1 billion valuation with your business idea isn't motivation; it's distraction. Focus on what delights you and the outcomes later. Jane Ann didn't set out to have a multimillion-dollar payday; she was simply reveling in creation. Tim Ballard wasn't focused on having his life story turned into a movie; he was pushed forward by the smiles of rescued children. Your journey might take you to outcomes even greater than you could have planned, but it's when you don't put limits on the outcome that all things become possible.

You're staring out at your new Frontier, but the possibility of future failure is creeping in. The comfort of your Charted Territory tries to pull you back. You hesitate. But this is the part where your journey begins; you face the fear and take the first committed steps across **The Bridge**.

CHAPTER 3

CROSSING THE BRIDGE

"If you're interested you'll do what's convenient. If you're committed you'll do whatever it takes."

—JOHN ASSARAF

When I was nineteen years old, I was called to serve a Mormon mission in Mexico. For those unfamiliar with the Latter-day Saints faith, a Mormon mission is a volunteer two-year calling that includes teaching about the church, service projects, and humanitarian aid. Up to that point in my life, the only time I'd been out of the country was an afternoon in Tijuana with my older brother. But I'd be rolling solo on this trip, no family at my side (I couldn't even call them unless it was Mother's Day or Christmas). Even though I was heading out into uncharted territory, I was excited to serve and to explore a new part of the world. After two months of training, which included intensive Spanish courses, I felt ready. As I walked through the airport, my last steps on US soil for the next two years, I thought, "How hard could this be?"

As soon as the wheels touched down in Monterrey, Mexico, I knew I wasn't in Kansas anymore. I collected my bags and went to meet my "comp." On Mormon missions, you travel in pairs, and your companion (comp) is assigned to work and live with you for several-month stretches before rotating. I would have several great companions throughout my mission, but numero uno didn't kick things off on a high note. He didn't speak any English, and I barely spoke Spanish. He had a scowl on his face the entire three-hour drive to the small village we'd be living in. No bueno.

The scowl transferred to my face when I went to bed that night. To stay cool, we had to keep our window open, which was essentially rolling out the red carpet for the hordes of mosquitoes waiting outside. I had to pull a sheet over my head so I wouldn't get eaten alive. A few hours before, it was, "How hard can this be?" Now all I could think was, "How did I end up here?" I couldn't talk with my roommate, and I couldn't phone a friend. Hell, my first letter took two and half months to get to the States. But somehow, the excitement was still bubbling underneath the fear; there was work to be done.

The next morning, our first appointment was with a

potential convert a few miles away. We rode bikes that barely deserved the name down an endless dirt road covered in rocks. Every hundred yards I was met with an overpowering smell that made me choke down vomit. I'd come to learn it was the smell of a dead, rotting dog (a companion I wouldn't get to switch out over the two years). Arriving at the house, the full weight of my uselessness set in. No one understood me. I didn't know where to sit. I was holding up a wall at best and making everyone uncomfortable at worst. A new thought crept in: "I'm going to die out here."

I was dripping with sweat and confusion when I somehow gleaned our last appointment of the day was with a girl who was about to get baptized. My mood shifted instantly, finally something positive. Since I was basically a paperweight in a suit, someone handed me a baby to keep occupied. She was covered in peanut butter, and very shortly I was, too. But it didn't matter; we were on a divine mission and my first spiritual win was around the corner. And then it all took a left turn. A domino effect of crying swept the room, first my companion, then the girl getting baptized, and then her family joined in. I understood without words it was time for us to go. I gave back the baby, the only other person besides me not crying, and we walked out. It turns out she had a change of heart and wasn't going to get baptized. I was devastated. I couldn't communicate or help in any way; I couldn't carry out the purpose of why I was there. I'd taken only a few steps on my journey, and I was ready to turn around.

As luck would have it, The Guide I needed would arrive the next day. The mission president, a senior leader in the church, would be doing one-on-one appointments with all the missionaries on his visit to our city. The timing was perfect as I was desperate for a pep talk. What I didn't know is our mission president was ex-military, a war general attitude with a middle-linebacker neck. He asked me how I was, and I unloaded all my insecurities and how hard my first day had been. I told him I felt wholly unprepared for what was being asked of me and I didn't think I was going to make it. I paused, ready for the warmth of a sympathy bath to rush over me, but what I got was a bucket of cold water thrown in my face. He slammed his desk and yelled, "DAMMIT, Elder Rex! I don't want any crybabies in this mission. You don't like it? Go work. You don't feel good? Go work. You miss your family? Go work. You can't speak the language? Go. To. Work. That's the key here: if something is bothering you, go to work. Now, get out of my office." I sat in stunned silence, eyes wide but my path clear. I got up, looked around the room for a second, and thought, "I guess I'm going to work."

When I walked out of that room, I was taking the first real steps of my journey—I was **Crossing the Bridge**. It was the point where I left my Charted Territory behind and consciously accepted the unknown of my new Frontier. I was leaving behind my comfort, my entitlement, and even my language. While a bit harsher than most of us need to get started, I had someone show me you can't get comfortable in a new world without being uncomfortable first.

The next two years were some of the best and most fulfilling of my life. From the vast unknown of a foreign country emerged my now familiar loves: work and service. There is a beautiful feeling at the end of the day when you know you've put in the work. There was an endless supply of things to do, and I was grateful and growing when I did them. I would end every day drained of energy, body aching, and emotionally spent, but when I pulled the sheet over my head, my heart and soul were full (a feeling no mosquitoes could touch).

The new territory of my life also showed me how to tap into an endless supply of love through service. Before my mission, I'd mostly done things in service of myself. But the Mexican culture showed me how to love beyond the confines of my own existence. They opened their homes and hearts, and I learned to embrace our differences instead of fearing them. I learned to speak Spanish, but I also learned to speak the language of acceptance. Years later on a trip to Jamaica, a tour guide turned to me and said, "You travel a lot, don't you?" I said, "Yeah, why?" He said, "Because I've never seen an American so comfortable in another country." Those years in Mexico made every country feel like home.

Like the first day of my mission, Crossing the Bridge into your new world will feel like you've arrived in a foreign country. The buildings will look strange, and you won't speak the language. You'll feel like an outsider, and you'll wonder why you ever left the comfortable place you came from. Most of all? You'll be afraid, but that's normal. Explorers, like the author Elizabeth Gilbert (*Eat, Pray, Love*), invite this fear. She knows trying to pretend you aren't scared is useless:

> "'Fear, you are part of the family of my consciousness. You are one of the emotions that I possess. And I hear your complaint, and I see your anxiety, and I see everything you're putting before me about how this will be a disaster, how I'm going to die, how everybody will mock me, how I'm going to fail, and I thank you so much for your contribution. However, your sister creativity and I are going to go off on this journey now and do this thing, but you're allowed to be in the car. We're going on a road trip, but I don't expect you to not come.' And once you allow fear to just be present, it seems to quiet down and go to sleep, and then you can go about your work. But it's never out of the picture, and I don't waste my energy trying to kick it out of the picture, because that feels to me like a colossal, exhausting waste of energy, whereas a radical, inclusive self-acceptance seems to be a way to be able to create a lot more." [1]

The stories in this chapter run the gamut of how those first steps over The Bridge can look—change in career, the passage from the games of youth to the adventure of adulthood, or the choice of values over fortune. Crossing the Bridge will expand your world forever; it never contracts.

Go to work.

PAYBACK (JASON SISNEROS)

Jason himself would admit his story is a cautionary tale, not one to be imitated. His early Charted Territory was one of abuse and trauma. Instead of watching cartoons as a kid, he would watch his mom being repeatedly beaten by his adopted father. He beat Jason, too, breaking his nose over a dozen times. But at nine years old, Jason did something he wasn't sure he was capable of. He stepped in front of his mom to take the blows. His adopted father hit him as hard as he could, but Jason didn't go down. It was a "good day," and the first time he ever felt strong.

Jason used his newfound outward toughness to hide his inner pain. He was drawn into gang life and drug dealing by the time he was twelve years old. A life on the streets was Jason's norm for years until the week his first son was born. When he looked down at his baby boy, he knew it was time to **Cross the Bridge** into the world of honest work. "My actions are going to affect him, and if I go out that way, that's the legacy I'm going to leave him and how he's going to grow up." Jason's crossing was a push into the unfamiliar world where disagreements were talked out instead of ending in bloodshed. On Jason's last drug deal before he went clean, he was stabbed in the chest (he still has a deep scar to show for it). But he survived, making it two births that week.

Jason's first real job was peeling the bark off logs for six dollars an hour. He soon "upgraded" to eight dollars an hour digging garbage out of a sump pump. It was a far cry from the easy money he was used to, and he was struggling to gain footing on the other side of The Bridge. "This was not a lifestyle I was used to, but I had my mind set on being a good man and making an honest living." He eventually worked himself into a position to buy his first company, but it was a short-lived triumph as his old ways sneaked in. "I couldn't pay my people. I needed payroll and this guy owed me a bunch of money, and my number one technique was to go and start flattening tires and breaking windows out of his heavy equipment." Jason had crossed over to his new world, but he still didn't understand the rules. He spiraled from one bad decision to the next and quickly found himself homeless on the beaches of Southern California.

At his lowest point, Jason found the key to his new world. A pastor at a homeless shelter gave Jason two books: *The Bible* and Tony Robbins's *Awaken the Giant Within*. "I took the Bible and tossed it. I told the pastor I'd already read it."

When Jason would get beat up as a kid, he'd get locked in his room until his bruises faded so he wouldn't draw attention. One of the only books in his room was *The Bible*. But Tony Robbins was new and unconnected to his past. When he read *Awaken the Giant Within*, he felt "a switch" turn on inside him. Jason realized for the first time the course of his life was in his control. "Up until then, it was all somebody else's fault. It made me feel good in the moment, but it didn't build any value or integrity or truth."

In a full-circle moment, Jason did his last drug deal to make the money to attend a Tony Robbins event. At the end of the event, there was a "special offer" to meet Tony in person if you signed up for the next event. It was in the day of credit card imprints instead of instant transactions, so Jason was able to put the sign-up fee on a card only he knew was maxed out. When it was his turn to meet his Guide, Jason looked up at Tony and told him, "I'm going to pay you back for this." Tony stepped back, his huge hands across his chest, and said, "I believe you." What Jason heard was, "I believe in you," and it was the first time anyone had ever looked him in the eye and said those words.

Not only did Jason keep his promise to Tony and pay him back, he kept his promise to himself and took control of his life. Jason is now a public speaker, entrepreneur, and philanthropist. His goal is to spark the change in others the way Tony did for him and create a legacy his son can respect. "It's not ever about our story; it's always about the people we're adding value to that may have gone through something similar and we become examples instead of a warning."

ELVIS NEVER GOT IN THE BUILDING (JASON HEWLETT)

Jason Hewlett spent decades honing his craft as a comedian and entertainer. He slogged through hecklers, lonely cruise ship gigs, and life on the road away from his family (including a not-so-festive Thanksgiving by himself at a taco stand). Jason was working so hard to "make it" that sometimes he wasn't even welcomed at home. After being gone for two weeks on the road, Jason opened up the front door expecting a big hug from his kids. "They ran right under my arm and went to Mommy. She had been gone for thirty minutes to get me from the airport." He wondered if all this was worth it.

Finally, the fame and fortune of Sin City came calling with a headlining show in Las Vegas. Jason's sacrifice was about to pay off. "I was offered a couple of different casino contracts, and they said, 'You're the next big thing in Vegas. We've brought in people like you that no one knew, and we've made them stars. You're next.'" But notoriety wouldn't come for free. In addition to a restrictive contract and a new manager, the show directors told Jason they needed to rewrite his show. "When I saw the productions they had created, they were not aligned with my mission statement in any way." Jason had two paths in front of him: compromise his values (family-friendly comedy) for "guaranteed success," or forge ahead with an aligned inner purpose and risk a career that might never feature stardom.

Jason had been faced with this decision once before and knew what he had to do. "A lot of people are making that choice in the moment. You need to make that decision a long time ago." Jason had picked his path when he was still a kid at a summer camp for singers and dancers. The camp culminated with a talent show, and Jason was ready with a "mean Michael Jackson" impression. The night of the show, Jason had the crowd eating out of his hand. When he went for a suggestive move, the crowd got louder and more excited. Jason decided he could bring the house down if he kept pushing it to the edge. "I did moves a kid should not be doing, especially at a church camp. The next thing I know, I'm doing a spin and ripping my shirt off while I fall to my knees. Standing ovation." Jason thought he had nailed it; the talent show victory was clearly his.

A triumphant Jason found an unhappy camp director waiting for him when he got off the stage. He'd been disqualified. Jason couldn't believe what he was hearing. "The director says, 'You know better than that; you were raised better than that. Why would you ever do that on this stage? You need to make a choice as to who you plan to entertain for.'

I wanted to punch him because what I did was good. But he was right. I had to make a choice. Do whatever people want, no matter how offensive, or be true to myself and my mission. And that's driven everything in my life since."

Instead of compromising his values, Jason crossed **The Bridge** away from fame and into a Frontier that mattered to him. With the distraction of hitting it big out of the picture, Jason had to face the harsh reality of how he was showing up as a father. When Jason tried to spend quality time with his son, he found himself easily distracted. A father-son lunch date to McDonald's brought his situation into sharp focus. "I slowly pulled out my phone and went to my favorite app, which was Facebook, and I'm scrolling through looking at what people had been eating and where they had been. Then I start posting this thing, saying, 'I'm on a daddy-son date at McDonald's. We're having a great time.' I realized what a hypocrite I was. I was like, what am I doing? I pressed down on the app and deleted it." When his son came down the slide and asked if they could play, Jason said yes and he meant it. "Instead of setting a goal to be a better dad, I made a promise to be the kind of dad any kid would want. Why set a goal when you can make a promise? You know if you miss a goal, you just reset a new one, nothing bad happens. But if you make a promise and you don't keep it, you have a real issue on your hands."

Jason kept his promise to himself and found success outside

of Las Vegas. Whether he's performing for thousands at an American Express corporate event or at a billionaire's private party, he does it with clean language and a clean conscience. "As a speaker, I integrate music, comedy, stories, impressions, but what ties it all together is this message about how we make a break or keep promises to each other. It's the highest level of engagement we commit to in any experience."

TRAIL MARKER #4

FIND THE DOOR THEY AREN'T GUARDING

In myth, a hero often encounters **Threshold Guardians** at the entrance to temples or gateways to new worlds. Their job is to assess those seeking entry and stop the unworthy. The non-myth world is full of Threshold Guardians as well—interviewers, lawmakers, loan officers, and even that giant of a man protecting the velvet rope at the hot new club. Technically, a Threshold Guardian isn't someone you invite on your exploration, but you'll need to learn how to deal with them nonetheless.

Threshold Guardians rarely bend to force, so you'll have to go around them. But the first step is recognizing you can go around them. Many people encounter some kind of authority or prevailing way of doing things and get stopped in their tracks. They prejudge themselves as "unworthy" to pass. Yet laws can be changed, entrenched industries can be disrupted and twenty dollars can be slipped to that surly bouncer at the door. Guardians are usually blunt instruments not designed to handle clever and determined Explorers.

The Threshold Guardians of Las Vegas stardom informed Jason Hewlett his act wasn't worthy of entering unless he made a few changes. Fortunately for Jason, they weren't guarding all the entrances to becoming a successful entertainer. He found another way in. I learned this powerful lesson in 2004 when the Boston Red Sox were on the verge of making a historic run to a World Series title. In game 6 of the ALCS, the Boston Red Sox beat the New York Yankees to tie the series 3–3. No one had ever come back from being down 0–3. And while I'm not a Red Sox fan, I've been a die-hard baseball fan all my life. The thought of seeing their eighty-five-year championship drought come to an end, in person, was something I had to do.

Many people would have conjured a hundred Threshold Guardians in their heads and put the opportunity out of their mind. Boston wasn't even in the World Series yet. They still had to beat the Yankees in game 7 the following night. It was 1:00 a.m. in Utah, and there were only a handful of flights that would get me there on time. I barely had any money to my name. I didn't want to go alone and would have to convince someone to join me on this last-minute adventure. So many Guardians—why even try? Because Guardians are only there to keep out the unwilling. I found a last-minute deal on a flight and a game 7 ticket for under $300. I called a friend in Cincinnati who picked up the phone in the middle of the night and agreed to meet me there. Eight hours later, I was in New York to see Boston complete their improbable comeback to make it to the World Series.

I could have stopped there, happy with what I'd overcome, but there were more Guardians in my future. I spent the weekend with my friend, during which Boston beat the Cardinals to take a 2–0 series lead. Games 3 and 4 would be in Saint Louis, only a four-hour bus ride from where I was. Here we go again. I arrived in time to catch game 3, another Boston victory, and they were one game away from vanquishing the famous Curse of the Bambino. I called my brother Dale, a huge Sox fan, and asked him to meet me in Saint Louis. I didn't have tickets yet, but after all I'd been through, I was sure we'd find them before the game. Except we didn't. There wasn't a scalper to be found in all of Saint Louis who had a ticket. The game was about to start, and the Threshold Guardians of the World Series loomed large.

I'd come too far to give up. We jumped in our rental car and drove up and down the streets around the stadium yelling out the window for anyone who had a ticket. When it seemed like all hope was lost, an unsuspecting Ally quite literally came out of the shadow of a building and said, "You want to get in the game? I can sneak you in." Apparently, he knew some-one who worked for Major League Baseball and had access to a special stamp which would let us bypass security if we paid him fifty dollars. As we approached the threshold with our "magic ink," we could feel some-one was about to get outwitted, but it wasn't clear if that someone was us. We held out our hands...and walked right in.

As the game was winding down, the Red Sox in the lead, their fans started moving down toward the edge of the field. As the final out was recorded and history made, I noticed people with special wristbands were being let onto the field to join the celebration. I made my way down to the edge of the field hoping one more Guardian would fall. It didn't look good as hundreds of police surrounded the field. That's when I heard him. "Larry! Hey, Larry!" There was a kid* next to me yelling at Larry Lucchino, the president of operations for the Red Sox. As Larry turned around, I threw my arm around the kid (who I didn't know) and joined in with his call, "Hey, Larry!" Larry looked into the stands and saw us, pulled a police officer to the side, and said, "Those two, let them on." The Threshold Guardian who was folded arms and stern looks a few seconds before was helping me onto the field to celebrate one of the most historic moments in all of baseball history.

A week prior, I was sitting on my couch thinking, "Wouldn't it be cool to go to game 7?" and here I was, throwing baseballs into the stands at the World Series. I held up the World Series trophy, hugged players, and made it on SportsCenter. My friend who had gone with me to the previous games called me, wondering if I was at the game. "At the game? Take a look at the pitcher's mound. I'm waving at you."

Most people would have been stopped at the gate, thinking the power of the Threshold Guardian couldn't be overcome. That might be true if you try to use force, but I didn't storm the gate or rush the field; I used my wits. So can you.

*If you were the kid yelling to Larry, please reach out. I owe you one.

THE BUCKET LIST FAMILY (GARRETT GEE)

As a freshman at Brigham Young University studying product design, Garrett Gee was frustrated by the pace of creating physical goods. "If you have an idea for a product and you design it, it's going to take years to get it to market. But in the world of software design and apps, you can have an idea, and a day later, weeks later, you can get that idea to market." To test the waters of software design, Garrett and a small team of friends built a mobile QR code scanner. He knew the market was already saturated with scanner apps, but Garrett thought they were slow and poorly designed. It felt like an easy warm-up before he dived into harder projects. He recalls thinking, "I'll start with my lame idea to get my hands dirty, learn some skills, and then I'll move on to my cooler ideas."

When the app was done, Garrett celebrated with a "big" launch party. "I guess my parties weren't cool; there were like twelve people there. I went around and made sure everyone downloaded my brand-new app." The next day when he met with the rest of the development team, Garrett proudly shared the news he'd gotten them their first dozen downloads. They laughed at him as they pulled up the analytics. Overnight, their app, Scan, had gotten 2,500 downloads. Their clean design cut through the crowded field, and the download rate continued to double every day until it reached 100,000 daily downloads. Then a million. Garrett's "lame" idea was a viral sensation.

As the downloads increased, so did the value of their app. This was in stark contrast to the modest ambitions the team had before they launched. "When we thought up goals, it was, let's try to reach a million downloads total, and let's try to sell it for $5,000. I can't even remember the third goal; it was so small. I remember thinking, I don't know who's going to pay us $5,000, but that would be sweet; that's good money." The team blew past their goal with $1.7 million in funding from Google in its first year. Year two garnered an appearance on *Shark Tank*, and although the Sharks passed, other venture capitalists put $7 million back into the company. Garrett finally let himself dream a little bigger: "Oh, we might be doing something for real here."

Garrett's senior year, things got real—a $40 million acquisition offer from Snapchat, but it wasn't without strings for Garrett. "Here's an acquisition for over $40 million on the table, but one of their stipulations was I needed to quit soccer right before my senior season. There was no way I was going to miss my senior season." Garrett envisioned his youth slipping away and wasn't ready to make such a grown-up decision. Without considering it any further, he followed his heart and told the Snapchat CEO, "Well, then, I'm sorry, we don't have a deal. I'm going to go play soccer." Garrett was halfway across **The Bridge** into the world of millionaire entrepreneur, but he turned around to settle on being a "college kid with an app."

While Garrett kept the door for soccer open, he had shut the door to the opportunities of a new Frontier. Luckily for Garrett and his entire team, his business partner wasn't going to let him stay within the walls of the settlement. In a frank conversation, he told Garrett, "I understand money is not your motivation in life and you have some well-rounded values, but you need to understand you're not the only person in this deal. You need to make it happen." Garrett realized his partner was right; he wasn't the only person he was impacting by settling and got the Snapchat CEO back on the phone to revive the deal.

With a multimillion-dollar fortune in hand, Garrett, now married, still didn't feel "grown-up enough" to decide what to do with that much money. "It didn't feel right to buy a house or cars or whatever, so my wife and I decided to do the opposite. Let's do a hard reset on life, sell everything, live out of suitcases, and do a trip around the world. Maybe we'll find a place where we want to settle down, but most of all, we'll learn from different cultures along the way and our experiences will tell us how we want to proceed with our future." With only a few hundred followers on social media, the only company who would sponsor their exploration was Teva. They gave Garrett some free sandals and wished him luck.

Eighty-five countries and three kids later, Garrett has done everything but settle. With millions of followers on social media and their pick of sponsorships (Airbnb, GoPro, Southwest Airlines), the Bucket List Family is forging new Frontiers across the globe. Having replaced his former

Snapchat salary with an online business, Garrett was able to use his windfall to support more than his family. "We decided we would only spend the money from the acquisition for humanitarian projects, charity, or to help others. When you travel around the world, you see opportunities all around you to do good." When the Bucket List Family heard about the devastation of human trafficking when traveling in Nepal, they knew they had to help. "We discovered one of the best ways to help these girls is providing them an education in a safe school, one with surveillance, giving them the confidence they need to avoid human trafficking." From their own contributions and those of their followers, they raised $50,000 to build a school in Nepal.

Aside from humanitarian projects, Garrett can't believe what he would have given up had he turned back to his Charted Territory. "My daughter's first day of school was at an orphanage in Bali. My little boy, who loves animals, learned what sound a lion makes by seeing a lion in person." And in a poetic turn of events, the choice to give up playing soccer at the beginning of his journey resulted in an unexpected outcome. When Garrett decided to leave Snapchat, only three months after the acquisition, there were still two days left before his senior season kicked off. He called the coach expecting it was too late but was surprised to be invited back. "The universe and the stars aligned for me and I ended up playing."

CROSSING THE BRIDGE WITHOUT FALLING OVER

You don't have to literally cross a border like I did when you take those first steps out of your Charted Territory, but it should feel like you've moved into a new world. Whether it's mental, physical, or financial, there has to be a "bridge" you cross signaling your commitment to the work. As Martin Luther King Jr. said, "Take the first step even if you can't see the whole staircase."

Your crossing won't be without fear. You're going to look down from The Bridge (even though you know you shouldn't!), see the rocks below, and decide it's not worth the risk. We're fragile in the face of a Frontier, responding with excuses and masking our strength so we don't have to use it. But when you stop looking for reasons to turn around and commit to the possibilities ahead, "doors will open where you didn't know they were going to be...doors will open for you that wouldn't have opened for anyone else" [3].

GET TRACTION

1. **Don't give in to resistance.** "Resistance," according to the author Steven Pressfield, is the force keeping us at lower levels of our potential [2]. This force can show up when we face a crossroads. Making a decision means you might make the "wrong one." So doing nothing feels safer. When Garrett Gee initially turned down selling his company, he was giving in to resistance. Explorers accept the discomfort of challenging resistance because when you turn away from your Frontier, you're refusing the "unlived life" within you.

2. **Prepare for the dip in the middle.** If you've ever crossed a swinging rope bridge and stopped in the middle, you'll be lower than when you started. Every exploration you undertake will have this dip as you make your way into the Frontier. Jason Sisneros dipped low as he crossed into the world of legitimate business, but each step forward put him on higher ground. When you're in the dip, you've got only two choices to get to higher ground: back to where you've already been or toward a new Frontier. Be brave. Pick the second path.

3. **Make a promise.** Jason Hewlett refused to cross the Bridge to fame and fortune because it would have broken a promise to himself. But he found another way into the Frontier, a path aligned with his values. There is always more than one Bridge into a Frontier, so pick the one where you can meet your goals without breaking your promises.

4. **Learn the language(s) of your new world.** Whether it's a spoken language like on my mission to Mexico or simply jargon specific to an industry, immersing yourself in the local lexicon is how meaningful progress is made. Don't expect to move into a new country, industry, or relationship and be successful without learning the prevailing modes of communication. Comfort, trust, and achievement come from nuance. Nuance gets lost in translation. Make becoming a "native speaker" in your new world a priority.

The first leg of your journey is complete. You've changed your mindset and left comfort in the rearview mirror. Now it's time to Adapt Your Body, to build the skills and muscle and calluses needed for the challenges ahead. **The Road of Trials** awaits.

PHASE II

ADAPTING YOUR BODY

When you first set out, you'll be inexperienced and unsure of what to expect. You'll start down the path and realize how unprepared you are, how uneven the road feels beneath your feet. You'll stumble and sometimes walk in circles, but your body will get stronger, your eyes will become sharper. The small hurdles you struggle over will build your confidence. The small wins will give you momentary glimpses of the bigger rewards ahead. This proving ground is called **The Road of Trials.** You'll emerge weary from the ups and downs but with the muscle memory of climbing over obstacles solidified.

CHAPTER 4

THRIVING ON THE ROAD OF TRIALS

"It's supposed to be hard; the hard is what makes it great."

—JIMMY DUGAN (PLAYED BY TOM
HANKS), *A LEAGUE OF THEIR OWN*

Have you ever had an experience in your life when the depth of your naivete is fully revealed? One of mine came when I went to apply for a winter semester at Brigham Young University (BYU). I'd finished my associate degree at a state college and figured the registration process was the same. I showed up three days before the semester started and asked the woman in the registrar's office where I could sign up for classes. She kindly informed me I needed to apply and be accepted first. I said, "Of course, that's what I'm doing." She disagreed and told me I had missed the deadline by four months.

With almost half a year to kill before I could apply again the right way, I needed something to fill my time. For lack of a better plan, I started listening to real estate training CDs (yep, CDs) a friend had given me weeks earlier. It took only a few hours until I had visions of a real estate mogul dancing in my head. A few months later, I was a licensed agent. I joined the brokerage of a family friend and showed up ready to pick up where the CDs left off. The team didn't want (or know how) to train me, so I was pointed to a desk and a phone and told to start making some calls.

At the same time, I was still trying to get the meat business to take off. I had twelve employees, three huge freezers of meat in my backyard, and strong sales, but we always seemed to be low on cash. Our lack of accounting systems didn't help to solve the mystery. What I did know for sure was the business had over $90,000 in debt and all of it was in my name. I'd taken out bank loans to buy refrigerated trucks, secure inventory, and hire a franchise lawyer in hopes of expanding. My personal credit cards were maxed, and I wasn't even taking a salary to help reverse the tide. As inexperienced as I was, even I could see this wasn't headed in the right direction.

With my hopes in the meat business fading and the debt piling up, I had to double down on real estate. Searching through my desk drawer one day hoping to find uncashed checks, I found a flier for a real estate seminar I had tucked away months earlier. It wasn't a check, but I was hoping it might pay off anyway. I showed up at the seminar wearing tattered jeans and my hat turned backward. I was a punk kid trying to hide a huge problem. What I lacked in dress, I made up for in attention. The seminar leader, Bill Pipes (now a lifelong friend and Guide), was laying out a real estate formula I knew I could follow.

After each day of doing the "homework," I was seeing results. I'd learned more in three days than I had in three months at the brokerage. I needed to figure out how to keep this going on an empty bank account. I went to Bill after the last class and told him how much I wanted this. I asked him to let me continue with the course and I would pay them back in two months. It was $1,000 a month I definitely didn't have and a Hail Mary I needed to be caught. Either he saw something in me or only wanted my money, but he let me stay.

After securing my spot in the real estate class, Herman, my partner, called me with more great news. He'd closed the $50,000 franchise deal we'd been working on for months. Before I even hung up the phone, I was mentally planning out the party for when I became a meat franchise millionaire. Not only were we saved, but we were also expanding. A few days later, $35,000 of the $50,000 disappeared from our account, and Herman disappeared with it. The party was over before it started.

Herman was the best salesman I've ever worked with. What I didn't know was, he was equally gifted at buying—mostly drugs. He finally showed up at my door two weeks later wearing the same clothes I'd last seen him in. "Jimmy, I'm so sorry, I'm a drug addict. The money is gone." I went from envisioning my name at the top of the "30 under 30" list to what felt like six feet under. I gave him a hug and said, "Do me a favor, I never want to see you again." I was twenty-four years old, $120,000 in debt, and an associate of someone who had committed grand larceny. I didn't want to go to jail, so I called the prospective investor and told him his money was gone and I needed sixty days to get it back.

I was faced with a choice: become bitter or get better. The company may have been done, but I wasn't. I made a red poster board of everyone I owed money to and how much and hung it on the wall. I would get up at 7:00 a.m., look at the board, and then get to work using the strategies I was learning in the real estate seminar. Day in and day out. Rinse and repeat. I was grinding so hard I'd often fall asleep in my suit. But it wasn't grinding me down; it was smoothing the edges. It was wearing away all my excuses and replacing them with the muscle memory of doing business the right way. The first month, I put twenty-nine homes under contract. The next month, I did thirty more. By the end of the full calendar year, I sold ninety-eight houses. I went from a nobody in the real estate world to one of the top salesmen in the entire state.

Two and a half years later, that red poster board was an office decoration, not a deficit. I had paid back every dollar of the $120,000. I often get asked how I sold so many homes when I first started in real estate. My response? Well, I kind of had to. I wasn't thinking, "I want to be the top real estate agent in Utah"; it was mostly, "I don't want to go to jail." Climbing over those hurdles honed my real estate skills at a pace I never would have achieved with less adversity. My reputation, my network, and my resilience were solidified in the wake of that failed business. What could have been my downfall became the path toward my greatest successes.

The obstacles and setbacks you'll encounter on your journey make up your **Road of Trials**. They're not the things happening *to* you but the things happening *for* you. As Campbell puts it, "All you have to do to transform your hell into a paradise is to turn your fall into a voluntary act. It's a very interesting shift of perspective and that's all it is...joyful participation in the sorrows and everything changes" [1]. You're going to get banged up and encounter people and circumstances that seem to be working against you. Either joyfully participate or get dragged down.

I had a difficult time selecting the people to highlight for this section because no one is immune to The Road of Trials. Not everyone struggles to identify a Frontier or Cross the Bridge, but *everyone* suffers defeats and setbacks along the way. The conversations I had with the following people stood out as true examples of the "joyful participation in the sorrow": brushes with death, enemies turned to allies, and the thousand pitfalls on the path to progress.

SAVED BY THE GYM (MIRANDA ALCARAZ)

When Miranda Alcaraz started doing CrossFit, it was "a bunch of weirdos in a warehouse throwing tires" and not the worldwide sensation it is today. Tired of her current workout, she followed an early CrossFit program she found online, but she didn't think it would hold her attention either. It turned out to be the most significant workout of her life.

The CrossFit road is hard. It's the type of workout you don't usually do on your lunch break and then head back to the office. You sweat a bucket and then puke into it. Miranda was instantly drawn to this challenge and was on the bleeding edge of CrossFit's development. "A lot of the movements I had never done before. In most gyms, you don't do cleans and snatches. Even back then, no one was doing burpees or anything. So we were learning how to do it by watching YouTube videos." Miranda felt the carryover of her intense CrossFit exercises into her real life. It was mind over matter to get through her workout. "No matter what I did for the rest of the day, this will have been the hardest thing."

Only a few years after discovering CrossFit, Miranda was

competing at a high level, traveling across the country to teach seminars and training for the national CrossFit Games. During one of those seminars in 2012, she went to get coffee for the rest of the trainers during a break. On the return trip, she encountered the first major hurdle on her **Road of Trials**, when a car going forty miles an hour slammed into her at an intersection. Her small rental car crumpled, and Miranda was rushed to the hospital. Luckily, the initial diagnosis wasn't terrible with only a broken hand and whiplash. The doctor gave her a soft neck brace and pain medication and sent her on her way.

After a week in pain, the "whiplash" wasn't going away, and Miranda knew something wasn't right. "I was in a lot of pain to the point where I couldn't brush my teeth. I had to sleep sitting up." She went to a new doctor who immediately ordered an X-ray. Seventeen days after her accident, they found the source of her pain—a broken neck. "They call it a hangman's fracture because it's literally the exact same break people have when they hang themselves. They told me if I would've tripped and fallen, or if I would've even gotten slightly rear ended, or sneezed wrong or whatever, I definitely would've been paralyzed for the rest of my life." It turns out those grueling hours in the CrossFit gym had saved Miranda's life. The doctors said her strong neck and shoulder muscles acted like an extra soft collar to stabilize the fracture.

Miranda fully recovered and was back at the CrossFit

Games on the leading team in 2015. "We were set to win, we had prepared so well, and we had such a great team." But the Road of Trials wasn't done with Miranda. With two days left in the competition, she suffered a torn ACL. Without all members competing, her team was disqualified, and Miranda was crushed. "I had given up so much in my life. I hadn't been working. I had my whole life wrapped up in winning the CrossFit Games and then it got taken away from us." The road didn't just feel hard; it felt like it had come to an abrupt and unsatisfying end.

With her competitive life over, Miranda shifted her focus to a career outside of CrossFit. She got a job at a supplement company and did workouts on the side. She also met her future husband, a CrossFit competitor as well, who lived several hours away from her. With both of them starting new careers, they ended up doing most of their workouts in his garage to save the time and energy of going to the gym. For fun, they'd post a simple workout from a hotel or garage to social media. The response was overwhelming and unexpected. Seeing an opportunity to give back to the CrossFit community, Miranda and her husband created a dedicated Instagram account for "regular people" to follow. She saw the need for something less intense than what was happening at the gym. "It doesn't need to be as complicated as you think. You can do CrossFit at home."

And then, you guessed it, another bump—a baby bump

this time around. As their project was taking off and a new mobile app in development, Miranda found out she was pregnant. "I thought the business was over. Nobody wants to see a pregnant lady showing you what to do for your workouts." Turns out she was wrong. The business thrived as they tapped into a key market—moms. Miranda doesn't think they come because the workouts are better for women, but because "they saw a real person, not these ripped women who don't seem to do anything but work out all day long." Far from pushing her off course, the bumps on Miranda's Road of Trials saved her life and built her business.

TRAIL MARKER #5

GO AROUND, NOT THROUGH, YOUR THRESHOLD GUARDIANS

Miranda helped people go around the Threshold Guardian of the CrossFit community by creating and sharing simple routines anyone could do at home. She released her viewers from ever needing to cross the threshold of a gym and to get what they needed outside of the system. I had my own clash with an entrenched system in 2017 when I took an adjunct teaching position in the business school at a local college. The pay wasn't going to be much, but it would be an easy way to give back to the community and hopefully make a difference to the students in my class.

I was prepared to write my own script as usual, when the director of the business school and a formidable Threshold Guardian, told me I had to follow the prepared materials for the course. She said I had about 10 percent discretion to fill in the gaps. I didn't challenge her; I smiled and told her I understood. Knowing this might be my only semester, I set out to teach from my experience, not the textbook. I wasn't going to be directly defiant but quietly nonconformist.

About three weeks into the semester, one of the students came up and asked me when I was going to input the grades into the system like all of his other classes. I told him I wasn't going to because in real life you don't always get a progress report and should do your best regardless. Plus, I didn't even know how to use the system to input the grades. At the end of the semester, I set up a meeting with the director of the business school to get a tutorial. When I told her I hadn't entered a single grade all semester, she was exasperated. "You can't do that!"

Well, apparently you could. I was ushered out after a short orientation on the system, and I assumed I would never hear from the school again.

Overall, I loved teaching the class, but as predicted, it would be my last. Even though the student evaluations said it was the best class they'd ever taken at the school and the director asked me to pick up two to three new classes for the next semester, I politely declined. I'd gone around this Threshold Guardian to give my students what I thought they needed, but I knew I couldn't stay in a system where I'd have to do that on a regular basis. So this book, my podcast, and my real estate coaching are how I share the tools I've gathered without the need of approval. You can do the same. You don't have to follow the rules of the prevailing system to have your unique voice heard. As Bruce Lee said, "Don't get set into one form; adapt it and build your own and let it grow. Be like water." Go around.

FACE EVERYTHING AND RECOVER (BRAD JENSEN)

Brad Jensen never felt like he quite fit in. "I came out of the womb restless, discontent. I was always on the outside looking in, kind of feeling this void inside." He tried filling the void with his first drink of alcohol at the age of twelve. "Once the feeling kicked in, I took a deep breath and it was like for a brief second, I was okay, just being Brad." Around the same time, Brad came across the world of nutrition and fitness. He would ride his bike to Barnes & Noble and sit for hours devouring every fitness magazine he could get his hands on. "It was the first time in my life I truly felt passionate about something. I even started creating my own meal plans." But he was a walking contradiction: packing tuna fish and brown rice sack lunches during the week and then chasing it with beer on the weekends.

Brad could see the empty calories of alcohol weren't going to help him achieve his fitness goals, but he still needed the escape. "The outside was starting to look better, but I still had this discontent in my soul." At a party his sophomore year of high school, Brad was offered pain pills instead of a beer. "That was the second thing in my life I've ever felt passionate about." The ratchet continued as "inside Brad" felt more and more disconnected. When the pain pills ran out one night, someone offered Brad heroin. He tried to refuse, he was above that sort of thing, but his friend insisted it would make him feel even better than the pain pills. Brad relented and crossed The Bridge into an uncontrollable new Frontier. "The first time I ever tried heroin, I went right to it and shot it up. I remember immediately feeling better, and the guy looked at me and said, 'Your life will never be the same kid,' and I'll never forget those words because it truly wasn't."

Brad spiraled into his new world, wreaking havoc on everything in his path. "Addiction is the great equalizer; it doesn't care. If you're black, white, purple, rich, poor, it doesn't care. Addiction doesn't discriminate." Brad sought help in rehab several times, managing one- or two-month stretches of sobriety, but "the pull was so great." His mom desperately wanted to help him and, as Brad recalls, "almost loved him to death." She kept bailing Brad out of jail and gave him money that went to more drugs. His dad knew what was happening and threatened to leave if she kept enabling him. Brad's strongest Allies were turning against each other.

After a year in jail, Brad had managed to build back some trust with his family. There was hope in the air as they planned a birthday party for him shortly after his release. "I came back, but I hadn't done any work. I'd been sober, but I hadn't changed who I was as a human." Brad made the call to his dealer the day before his party. "I got into the car, and I was crying the whole way there because I knew what was next. I know what happens when I start using: everything goes down. I didn't show up to my own birthday party the next day."

Brad finally got the help he needed when his family cut him off. "My parents telling me 'We love you, but until you want to get sober, we can't have you around' was the best thing that ever happened to me." The **Road of Trials** would dip deep into a valley before it came back up again. Brad escaped from a rehab hospital in a gown and no shoes and started walking down the side of a busy freeway. When the cops pulled up beside him, he insisted they had the wrong guy. "I thought I just had a problem with heroin. What I found out was, I had a problem with everything. I had a problem with Brad. I didn't know who I was as a person and I kept looking for something to numb that."

For the next eleven months, Brad pushed through the most dangerous territory of his life. He fell in with a group of white supremacists, was in and out of five rehab centers, and spent more time inside jail than out. But there were no more safety nets, no more bailouts. "It was God finally allowing me to not just hit rock bottom but to sit in it." The path Brad was traveling led him to look inside and face the underlying issues. "The drugs stopped working. I couldn't put enough drugs in me to fill the hole, and that's when I decided to make a change."

On November 20, 2012, Brad was let out of jail to attend his grandfather's funeral. On the way back, he told the cop he was excited to go back; this would be the last time. The cop laughed. "Do you know how many times I've heard that from the back of a cop car?" Brad laughed, too. "Do you know many times I've said that from the back of a cop car?" But this time was different. Brad was out of jail shortly after, holding all his worldly possessions in a garbage sack—one shirt and one pair of pants. "I went to an Alcoholics Anonymous meeting and I remember thinking, I'm going to get back doing what I love, and it was never a question."

Brad set to work slowly building credibility in the fitness

and nutrition world. He put in time at smaller gyms as a personal trainer, while attending seven Alcoholics Anonymous meetings a week to stay on track. His clientele grew to a point where it made sense to start his own business. Even though everyone around him knew he was ready to build something on his own, the fear still crept back in. "I remember thinking about the fear acronym. You can either face everything and recover or F everything and run." Brad's Road of Trials had prepared him to face the fear. Eight years after his last ride in a cop car, Brad is the owner and founder of Key Nutrition, a fitness and nutrition company supporting over 200 clients a week. "I absolutely have a love for helping people and seeing the light come on. It was huge for my early recovery to see I could make a difference in someone else's life. I was a taker my whole life, and now it's time to give back."

THE STRUGGLE ISN'T YOUR STORY (JUSTIN PRINCE)

After his parents divorced, Justin Prince's mom laid out the stark reality of their new Charted Territory. With Monopoly money in hand, she lined up Justin and his siblings and started counting. "This is how much our rent costs. This is how much our utilities and groceries cost. She kept lining up the bills, and there was no more Monopoly money." Even as his mother laid out the cold, hard facts, Justin still envisioned a better life for himself. "Even as a little kid, I was a dreamer. I was like, one day, I'm going to be somebody."

Justin got his first taste of being somebody by selling cartoon bible movies at a shopping mall kiosk. Although his initial sales numbers weren't great, he was quickly learning the rules of this new Frontier. "I was learning how to work hard and how to keep a good attitude even through rejection. Eventually, I became the most successful salesman the company had had in over thirty years." But Justin didn't feel like "somebody" yet, and he wasn't about to settle. "Most of us lead kind of mediocre lives. We're not happy with what we're doing, but it doesn't hurt bad enough to do anything about it."

Justin left the Charted Territory of the mall kiosk and became a top three salesman and the national spokesman for his next company. He was flying high as usual, with no end in sight. So when the company unexpectedly went out of business, the fall came hard. "One day, I was the man; the next day, I was not." With a baby at home and his wife pregnant with another, the climb back seemed steeper than ever. Ever the dreamer, Justin started working on a side business and went back to selling anything he could. "I had a car full of twenty-five-year shelf life food storage, animated bible movies, and then this little part-time business I'm building. I'm telling people, we can do this." Justin would not let **The Road of Trials** be the end of his journey.

Justin figured he'd be a full-time entrepreneur in a matter of months, but the reality was ten times longer. He kept himself motivated by repeating his daily mantra: "Your struggle is not your story. How you overcome the struggle is the story." Justin saw many people around him let the struggle become the story of their life, which ultimately led to quitting. But retreating to the safety of mediocrity was never an option. "There are always reasons to quit, and there are always reasons to keep going. The reasons you choose will define you."

When he became an equity partner in a failing twenty-five-year-old beauty products company, Justin would have no shortage of reasons to quit. But as he dug into the assets and opportunities of the company, Justin saw how he could overcome instead of owning the struggle. "The most sacred thing in business is opportunity. People look for it their whole life. They'll get under the fence in the middle of the night, in the middle of the desert to find opportunity. People yearn for it." Grasping the opportunity was not going to be reaching for low-hanging fruit but a long, grueling, and uncomfortable turnaround. "Comfortable is self-preservation. Just sit there and don't get hurt. But all of the juice in life is outside of that comfort zone." Justin willingly signed up for the struggle.

Justin was in the trenches, building sales teams, taking long trips away from his family to learn new markets, but knowing all along the trials would be worth the payoff. "One of the hardest things to do in business is a turnaround because there's already an existing culture. Changing the engine of a 737 when you're at 30,000 feet is not easy. That's the hardest. The second hardest thing is the startup. We literally did both at the same time." In 2014, the startup, Modere, launched in the US. The following year, they launched in twenty-nine countries. Two years after that, the former "sinking ship" was bringing in hundreds of millions of dollars in revenue.

Looking back, Justin believes his motivation for pushing through his Road of Trials came from outside himself. He remembers looking at his son in his car seat in the rearview mirror and saying to himself, "I want to make that little kid proud. I want him to grow up and be proud of his dad. I want to make my wife proud. That was a driving force not to quit, to work through it, overcome obstacles, and develop into a leader." In the end, the bumpy road didn't grind Justin down; it shaped him into the person he was striving to be. "Adversity is where you build your compassion and build your empathy. It's where you build your humility; it's where you build your relatability." Big dream, big struggle, big victory.

OPENING NEW DOORS (SETEMA GALI)

Watching a flag football game in kindergarten, six-year-old Setema Gali knew he'd found his first Frontier. "There was like this ignition, this spark of, I want to do that." The future he envisioned was so real that he felt like he could reach out and touch it. "BYU football helmet on, mud all over my uniform, waving to the crowd." When ninth grade rolled around, Setema committed to making his dreams a reality. "It was my first experience with setting goals and writing them down in a journal. One goal was, 'Get a college scholarship to Brigham Young University.' I became very hungry. I don't know what it was, but I wanted it; I wanted to play.'"

Bolstered by a four-inch growth spurt and a dedication to the weight room, Setema went from a 165-pound high school benchwarmer to a 205-pound freshman at BYU. "I wasn't the fastest, I wasn't the strongest, but I had this mantra that said, 'I can work. You give me enough time, and I'm going to beat you.'" And work he did; another year in the weight room pushed Setema from 205 pounds to 245 pounds. "I went out with my high school buddies, and they were like, 'Dude, are you on steroids?' I was like, 'No, I just know what I want.'" Setema's first goal had been checked off, but his football journey wasn't yet complete. He was a freight train headed straight for the NFL.

Setema joined the New England Patriots as an undrafted free agent and spent two seasons under the legendary coach and Guide Bill Belichick. "I've had some amazing coaches and mentors. A lot of my success has come down to working with coaches, mentors, people who I can model my life after, model my language after, and get coached. Any other athlete or actor or person who's trying to do something big, they'll have coaches." As a defensive end on the practice squad, Setema contributed to the beginning of a football dynasty, as the Patriots won the Super Bowl in 2002. But the high was followed by a big low as Setema was cut by the Patriots weeks before the 2003 season. His life as a football player was over, and the next Frontier looked uncertain. "When you finish football and all you've done is football, it's like, 'What do I do now? What do I do with my life?'"

One look at the paycheck of a friend working as a mortgage lender was the easy answer Setema needed. He moved full speed ahead, starting in mortgages, then to real estate developments and hard money deals. Like so many others, Setema found himself on the wrong end of the real estate bubble when the market collapsed in 2008. "I wasn't ready for it. It's like we hit the bottom and then went to the basement of the bottom." He couldn't even stay in the basement of his own home as he hadn't paid the mortgage in seven months. Traveling **The Road of Trials**, Setema's family lived out of suitcases, bouncing from couches to foreclosures and selling everything they owned. Almost everything.

The savior of Setema's family had always been close at hand (quite literally). With no other options, Setema's wife came to him and said, "There's something you have that's very valuable." "And I looked at my Super Bowl ring, and I'm thinking, I gotta do what I gotta do to feed my family." Setema found a collector in New York who wanted to buy the ring. He had to borrow the money to fly there and "cried like a baby all the way to the airport." While the money from the ring rescued them from financial ruin, Setema was barely hanging on. "I was overweight, depressed, angry at life, angry at God." Setema had to look in the mirror and challenge his own story. "You made all this money, and now this is it? You're going to settle? I knew God had created more for me, this was all part of the journey, and I wasn't going to let this define me; I was going to let it refine me."

In 2011, Setema began knocking on doors in hopes one of them would open. Taking a job selling security systems, Setema was dropped off in a neighborhood as a trainee having never sold anything in his life. There was no other choice. He thought to himself, "I've got to do this for my wife and for my kids. I've got to learn how to sell, how to knock on a door, how to get in a home, I gotta figure this thing out." When everyone else had gone home that first day, Setema was working through the night. At 9:30 p.m., Setema walked up the steps of the last house with the words he'd left with his family repeating in his head: "Daddy's going to work harder than anybody. I will outwork everybody, I promise you." Delirious but determined, Setema got the last sale of the day. "I knew my life was meant to be more than some success in the NFL and some success in mortgages. I couldn't see myself settling and fading off into oblivion. So I knocked. If you do hard things, you get results. You get muscles, and your confidence grows into certainty."

Setema knocked on doors for three more years before the Frontier of coaching crept onto the horizon. "I started to get these feelings—very strong, distinct feelings. I call it the Voice. And the Voice was basically like, 'Okay, it's time.' And the answer was to go and do what I do now, which is to coach." Drawing on the world-class coaches he had in the past and surrounding himself with new expertise, Setema built his muscle as a leader. He was learning how to "win after the game." Setema is back on top as one of the leading speakers and coaches in the country. His mission is to reach out to others struggling like he did and help them listen to their "Voice." He wants his clients to be confrontational—not fighters but people who face the facts like he did. He pushes them up the steps so they can knock on the door. "You can work your way out of things, you can figure things out, but you've gotta be in action."

HOW TO TURN A ROUGH ROAD INTO TOUGH FEET

My business mantra for the past decade has been, "The difference between successful and unsuccessful people is successful people have merely learned to do the things unsuccessful people don't want to do." Explorers learn to do the hard things. They're willing to follow their Road of Trials into the swamp, to do the things most people are unwilling to do, and create the experiences, relationships, and empathy to sustain them on the rest of the journey.

The initial excitement propelling you forward will eventually fade away and will be replaced with the monotony of hard work and bouts of failure. You'll believe uphill is the only terrain you'll ever see again. But as Maslow put it, "We must be quite ready, not only to beckon forward, but to respect retreat to lick wounds, to recover strength...so that courage for growth can be regained" [2]. Your capacity is always bigger than the challenge, but it's the challenge that makes it accessible.

GET TRACTION

1. **Prepare yourself for a struggle equal to the size of the reward you seek.** If you want a big payoff, be ready for an equally rocky road like Justin Prince. Most people want a big dream, a small struggle, and a big victory. They want to win a million dollars in the lottery instead of getting to the same place with years of hard work. In the end, the latter has a better chance of happening, and you'll have earned the wisdom of work along the way.

2. **Face the facts and recover.** When you hit those first bumps and sharp edges on the Road of Trials, you can either face them and recover or "F everything" and run. Like my pile of debt or Brad's addiction, you have to look your adversity in the eye to overcome it. Accept and recover.

3. **Put in the reps.** The Road of Trials is the Explorer's version of boot camp. You practice swinging across a shallow mud pit to prepare you for when there's nothing but a hundred-foot drop below. You put in the reps so you're ready for the bigger lifts. Miranda Alcaraz put in the reps, preparing her body and her mindset to carry her through the setbacks.

4. **Keep knocking until the right door opens.** When everyone else has gone home for the night, you've got to keep knocking. Your persistence on The Road will pay off like it did for Setema Gali. Not every door is meant for you, but you won't find the right one if you walk away too early.

The Road of Trials is now behind you. You adapted to the ups and downs the outside world threw at you and came out on the other side—level and stronger. Now for the inner work. The twisted paths within you are usually the last you'll want to explore. Yet the final steps of your journey need a complete Explorer, prepared inside and out. You can't go around it any longer, it's time to enter **The Cave.**

REVEALING YOUR HEART

The outer challenges of the Road of Trials subside, but the inner challenges rise and threaten to overtake them. The fight with your internal dragons happens in **The Cave**. This will be your most mentally taxing test, a battle with all the insecurities and doubt and unworthiness you've collected along the way. But once cast off and left behind, you'll emerge from The Cave with a clear mind and the courage to show your true self to the world.

With a trail-tested body and the depths of your heart explored, you'll stand before your final climb. All your hard-fought knowledge and perseverance will be put to the test as you push for the summit. This is called **The Mountain**. Unlike the long and winding path of The Road, The Mountain has no other way but up. It's the final test to separate the wanderers from the true Explorers.

At the peak you'll discover, and be truly worthy of, an invaluable treasure. It's likely not what you sought when you began, but it's a prize you'll carry with you forever. Everything you've overcome and suffered through will have transformed who you are. This is **The Reward**.

CHAPTER 5

ENTERING THE CAVE

"A single candle can both defy and define the darkness."

—ANNE FRANK

Who am I? At thirty-three years old, that was the question keeping me up at night and nagging me throughout the day. I could have answered myself by saying, "You're a successful business owner. A dedicated uncle. An involved community member," but what always came out was, "You're a fraud." I was ashamed of who I wanted to be and racked with guilt about who I wasn't.

I had grown up in a devout religious community and household, with well-defined expectations of how my life should look. But those expectations didn't match what the core inside of me felt. My outside world looked put together, but my inside world was a mess. I wasn't fitting the mold of what a returning Mormon missionary should be and do. I hadn't gotten married, and I certainly wasn't raising children in an eternal family. So who was I?

I didn't want to be a victim of my circumstances and vowed to take charge of understanding who I needed to be. To make something right, you have two options: make the other person or thing "wrong" or look inward and make a change. What I learned on my mission (ironically) was, I was not a victim. If I wanted to figure this out, I had to "go to work." I began working with different life coaches who could help me navigate this overwhelming change. For the first time in my life, I turned inward and asked, "Why are these my standards?"

I started traveling more and meeting people who didn't fit the mold of what I had been taught a "good" person looked like. I was introduced to beautiful, loving people who wouldn't have been accepted by my religious community. They drank alcohol, had sex before they were married, were LGBTQ, or a combination of all three! They were interesting and vibrant and unfettered by their choices. And contrary to my experience, they didn't use their lifestyles as instruments of judgment. I was accepted by them, no questions asked. The only expectation was love and acceptance in return. I was being shown another way.

The next year and a half of my life was an exploration of what it meant to be spiritual. What was "God"? What was the Mormon church? How is spirituality different from religion? After over 800 hours of study, I concluded everything I believed to be true...wasn't. I had opened a hole in myself I wasn't sure I could close. Everything I had built my life on, what I believed to be my "purpose" on Earth and what happens after my time on Earth, was paper thin. I held my belief system up to the light and I could see right through it.

When I looked directly at the rawness of who I wanted to be, it was shocking and liberating in equal measures. There was another person hiding inside of me who finally got to step out and stand on his own. Campbell refers to this as the inner battle. You believe you're only heading out to conquer the world, but you realize you also have to slay yourself. My life coach, Melissa, an essential Guide in my life, was critical in helping me let go of the shame forcing my other self to stay hidden. After a particularly bad rejection by a woman I was dating, I went out the next night and hooked up with someone I had just met. I woke up the next morning with an intense shame hangover, and I thought Melissa was going to berate me on our next call. Instead of judging me, she released me. "Were you kind to her? (Yes.) Was her life worse off having met you? (No.) Did you think her intention was different from yours? (No.) Jimmy, you didn't do anything wrong. She got what she wanted and so did you." The shame and the guilt melted away. It wasn't all black and white but a world filled with messy, complicated, beautiful gray.

That messy gray extended to my spiritual life as well. I knew I still believed in a higher power, something bigger than myself, but I didn't know how to reconcile my belief with a blank slate. On one of the many dark nights praying for clarity, my aha moment showed up. Love. What was the one thing Christ taught when he was here on Earth? To simply love other people. If I spent my entire time on Earth trying to love other people, trying to bring happiness to others, then any all-knowing, all-loving God is going to honor that regardless of what church I walk into or out of. I solidified this new moral code at a Tony Robbins "Date with Destiny" event where I wrote my life's purpose:

> *To share my tremendous love with all of God's children, bringing happiness to others through my playful soul and by being an example of leading an extraordinary life.*

Emerging from that dark period wasn't all filled with light. My whole family and most of my best friends were still part of the culture and religion I had moved on from. I had changed, but that didn't mean those around me would be ready to embrace the new me. At least now I felt like I could be with them authentically, whether they accepted it or not. What had been solidified for me in years of sometimes painful inner work was being who you are is a gift and shouldn't be guilted away from you. I knew this all too well because before I let go of my own guilt and shame, I was doing my fair share of piling it on others. I cared more about *what* people were doing in their lives against my moral code and less about *how* people were doing on this everyday struggle we all face. When I stopped judging what others needed to be, I could love people (myself included) for who they were.

At some point along your journey, you'll come face to face with your own inner battle, a dark place only you can enter. This is **The Cave**. There is no Guide who can drag you in. There is no Ally who can stand up and take your place. "Each one has to work it out in his own way" and do the hard, inner work of learning to "recognize your own depths" [1]. The Cave is not a mountain or river you can navigate around. The Cave is something you have to willingly go into, not knowing what it will take to get out.

Entering the Cave is the hardest test an Explorer will face. You're up against a foe who knows all of your weaknesses, who knows all of your fears and the secret shame you've never spoken. You'll grope around in the darkness feeling like the real you isn't enough to finish the challenge. The real you isn't strong enough, smart enough, deserving enough for the path you've chosen. But entering The Cave will mean the end of who you were before. And when the mask is lifted, the face staring back at you will be whole.

The Explorers you'll read about next all found the "proper field of battle is not geographical but psychological" [2]. They went into the Cave with packs weighted by anger, shame, and judgment and emerged lighter, their accumulated burdens left behind. You can't go over it. You can't go under it. You've got to go into it.

RIPPING YOURSELF OPEN (SEAN WHALEN)

Even as a little kid, Sean Whalen was a businessman. "I was the kid who went around door to door and asked if I could mow the grass for five bucks. I'd take the five and I'd give my little buddies two so we would all have ice-cream money when the truck came." By the time Sean was twenty-five years old, he'd turned that mentality into a multimillion-dollar fortune servicing mortgages in the housing boom. Instead of ice cream, he was buying sports cars, Rolex watches, and a 9,000-square-foot house. But without any strong Guides to keep him balanced, Sean figured this Charted Territory would stretch on forever. "I didn't understand coaches. I didn't understand mentors. I read tons of books, I tried to surround myself with smart people, but I was all ego. I was arrogant. I had a ton of money and thought I would continue to win."

Nevertheless, Sean felt like he was "juggling bowling balls" trying to maintain his streak of success. "I'm running around burning the candle at both ends working a hundred hours a week. I haven't been to my kid's soccer game in who knows how long, but technically I'm successful based off all this materialistic shit I have, but it's not making me happy." When the housing market crashed, all the balls dropped. "I lost millions of dollars; I went through a divorce and bankruptcy. It was the ultimate explosion; everything came apart at the same time."

The candle burned out, and Sean was engulfed by darkness. He charged into the depths of his unhappiness fueled by rage. "I was mad, I was angry, but I didn't know who I was angry at." For years, he was telling everyone he was "good," he was "fine." In reality? He was drowning. Sean was fighting the image of what he thought a man was supposed to act like, an image he couldn't sustain. With the help of a friend who had gone through something similar, Sean pushed past his surface emotions and into **The Cave**. It felt like "ripping myself open and realizing this is who I am; I'm real and I am afraid of certain things."

Emerging from The Cave, Sean was raw but reflective. The questions he didn't have time to ask before suddenly felt more urgent than ever. "Why am I doing all of this? What does this mean? What am I after? What brings me the most joy?" The answer he kept coming back to was freedom. His previous life of hundred-hour workweeks and fast cars had him speeding in the other direction. "I didn't control my time; I didn't control anything." Most of all, Sean wanted the freedom to be vulnerable for the first time in his life. "We walk around every day bullshitting everybody, not telling the truth on social media, not telling the truth to our lovers, our significant others, to our kids, to our families, and to our friends. I started telling my truth and telling people how I felt. I started sharing who I was, and I started letting out the darkness."

Sean's consulting business, Lions Not Sheep, was born from this unapologetic drive to be real. The name came from a desire to give a voice to "Sean 2.0." He made a T-shirt that said, "Lions Not Sheep," not intending it to become a movement or company, but the message resonated across social media. "Come to find out everybody is dealing with their own thing in one way or another. The more you share, the more open you are, the more liberating it is. I want freedom. I want light. I don't want to be sitting around with a backpack full of rocks." The movement was an overnight sensation, as high-profile entrepreneurs, fathers, and people on the verge of suicide were drawn to Sean as he publicly unloaded his rocks and took control of his life. "I can follow along with everyone else who is miserable and broke, or every move, every decision. I can shine my light, be this lion."

Becoming the Guide he missed early on, Sean is coaching people to face the fear of judgment. His clients aren't afraid of risk or change or failure; those are easy. "Most people I talk with are afraid of judgments." And that's where a Lion doesn't care. "When you think about it, you're going to be judged either way. No matter who you are, no matter what you are, no matter where you are. So why not lighten your burden?" When you put down the rocks, you walk taller in the world.

THE OTHER SIDE OF DISCOMFORT (BAYA VOCE)

Baya Voce was a cast member on the twenty-first season of MTV's long-running reality show *The Real World*. After a year with seven strangers and some distance from the cameras, she thought, "Why did I do that? That was such a strange thing to do." Not content to shrug it off as a youthful call for attention, Baya dug deeper to uncover her motivations. "There was this real lack of understanding about myself and a real lack of community in my life. I was craving it in any way I could find it." One of the ways Baya satisfied her craving growing up was to be popular, doing whatever it took to be part of a community. Her Charted Territory was built on false assumptions and unmet needs.

The more questions Baya asked herself, the fewer answers she seemed to find. She had lost control of who she was and who she wanted to be. "All of a sudden, I don't even know who I am anymore. I don't have a sense of self because my sense of worth has been created by everybody around me." All of Baya's decisions became fair game for exploration. A flippant "look at me" social media post would later end up under her self-reflective microscope. What felt like a harmless way to share things about her life was coming from a deeper place of insecurity. Her online life was being created for "assurance and validation from the outside in."

Baya landed back in Utah in her early twenties, looking to create more authentic relationships. "I came back single, but people in Utah get married a little younger and the dating scene was terrible. I was having such a hard time meeting people because everybody I knew was married." Baya wasn't going to be a victim of her circumstances, so she set to work to solve the dating landscape herself by hosting her own events and mixers. "I wanted to see if I could help make the dating scene cooler for people who weren't married at twenty-four." While Baya didn't find "the one" during those events, she did build a strong network of interesting, single people who began reaching out to her for dating advice. "I started matchmaking. But the problem was, I would set people up and what would happen over and over again is the guy would call and say, 'That was the best date. I can't wait to go out with her again.' And the woman would call and say, 'I never want to see that guy again. That was a terrible first date.' Where was the disconnect?"

Baya's feelings of disconnection were clearly not unique, so she set out to find the source. She sprinted across The Bridge into the new Frontiers of psychology, emotional intelligence, body language, and neuro-linguistic programming (NLP). Baya's most accessible study subject was herself, and she began digging to find the root of her feelings of incompleteness. Where most people enter **The Cave** with reluctance and only when pushed to the brink, Baya entered willingly with a clipboard in hand. Even though difficult and sometimes painful, Baya was fascinated by who she met "on the other side of discomfort."

Her research and introspection ultimately pointed to a pervasive feeling of isolation. She felt the loneliness and isolation in the world was caused by people pushing down their inner "cravings or the things we desire," which impacted the quality of their relationships. "Oftentimes, our desires are not things that are allowed in everyday society. And because they're not talked about, we feel like we're the only people who feel a certain way and somehow, we're wrong for that." Baya wanted to normalize these hidden desires and bring them into light. She wanted to take the cravings that make us feel alone and "bring them into experiences that are fun, in a place that feels safe."

Not only has Baya made connection and safely accessing desires a way of life, she's also built it into a business. Through high-concept "experience design," Baya is helping people get to the other side of discomfort by willingly entering The Cave. "Whether that's designing a ritual to grieve the loss of a relationship or a dinner party to inspire guests to unlock dormant sides of themselves," she wants to draw people out of isolation. "If we commit to letting transition be our teacher, our guide, even our muse...it will be the biggest gift we ever give ourselves." Millions of people have been inspired by Baya's message as her TEDx Talk, "The Simple Cure for Loneliness," is one of the most popular talks on the platform. "Rituals can serve different purposes. Some rituals serve the purpose of community; some rituals serve the purpose of coming back to yourself, self-development. Rituals go back to your health; you can have rituals for anything. I focus on rituals that create connections."

EXCUSES ARE A PRISON (KYLE MAYNARD)

Kyle Maynard is a speaker, author, former GNC World's Strongest Teen, and an MMA fighter. He also happens to be a quadruple amputee, born with a rare condition called congenital amputation. Being born without limbs could have easily led Kyle to have limiting beliefs about Frontiers that were accessible to him. Fortunately for Kyle, his family and friends knew he could be an Explorer, and they helped lay out an expansive territory for his future. His grandmother would often tell him, "Kyle, when people hear your voice and they see your face, the disability will fade away."

The Frontiers Kyle pressed into seemed without end. His mantra became, "To know our limits, we have to test our limits." He wrote a *New York Times* best-selling book, entered MMA competitions, opened a CrossFit gym, joined the Washington Speaker's Bureau, and was the first quadruple amputee to climb Africa's highest peak without assistance. Kyle attributes tackling these "impossible" challenges to the mindset he had growing up. "When you're a kid, you don't know the limitations yet that the world can put on you."

Eventually, the limitations came but from Kyle himself. "When I first started speaking, I didn't feel worthy of it. I was making a ton of excuses, and I wasn't taking care of myself. I was traveling nonstop and I was lonely. I became this depressed motivational speaker, and I was ready to quit." At the airport on the way to an event, Kyle thought it would be his last. "I went through security, and I saw a couple guys who were looking at me. I went over to shake their hand, and I saw one of them was badly burned. They had been in an ambush in Iraq. They told me they saw my story on TV and it helped them get through some dark times. That completely reframed it for me and changed my perspective." The Road of Trials was rough, but the payoff of being a Guide for others was worth the pain. "We can make a difference in people's lives, and it's not always about having the biggest or best platform, it's not about having the most likes on Instagram. It's about the depth of connection to those who are listening, that their life might go a different way because of something you said."

Reinvigorated by his purpose, Kyle expanded his business,

taking on substantial risk in the process. "I wanted to start and build something and I didn't even know necessarily what it was. I had this faith I'd be able to do it, but I wasn't patient and I wasn't strategic. I fell flat on my face. I had to fire several people." For five months, Kyle retreated from the world. "I was in hell. I was so caught up in what I should be doing. I didn't call friends; I was noncommunicative. I'd been to all these heights, but then all of a sudden, I had to reexamine everything."

Kyle had focused his life on outer achievements but had avoided his inner depths. "I quit believing in the message I was sharing, and I needed to face some hard truths." Kyle went into **The Cave** not only to examine his present circumstances but also to let go of the past. "I had a lot of shame and guilt for wanting to take my life when I was ten years old. That time period felt so permanent and so real. It never is; it always passes. But the arrow of time moves one way, and yet the direction of our lives, of the growth or recession, can move both ways."

Kyle didn't like everything he found in The Cave, but it was the hard truths that pulled him back out to keep exploring. "It doesn't make me a good or bad person because of the way I was born. The only way to look at yourself is to be unafraid of what you'll see. It's not so good sometimes. That shadow exists within all of us. It's not something to be taken away or suppressed. It's to be integrated into who we are." Kyle is content to accept a path that has some twists and turns. "It's not always an upward trajectory. It can be messy and ugly and feel cruel and unusual. But for those of us who can inspire others to speak their truth and live their truth, it's our role."

THE BIRTH OF THE IRON COWBOY (JAMES LAWRENCE)

The night after James Lawrence ran his first marathon, he needed a wheelchair to get around. He wasn't injured; he was out of shape. "There are millions of runners out there who do this pain-free. Why was I in so much pain? It was because I wasn't strong enough. I didn't have enough experience." Ten years later, James accomplished an athletic achievement that will likely not be duplicated. The "Iron Cowboy," as he's come to be known, completed fifty Iron Man triathlons in fifty days in all fifty US states. That's 120 miles of swimming, 5,600 miles of biking, and 1,311 miles of running. No days off, no rain delays, no excuses.

James came up with the "50/50" in the wake of the 2008 housing collapse. His Charted Territory was turned upside down as he lost his house and everything in it. "I could still be wallowing in that loss or turn it into an opportunity, a turning point in my life." A new Frontier as the world's most ambitious endurance athlete came into view. "I knew if I got on the other side of the 50, doors would open. I didn't know which ones and I didn't know how many, but that became the massive driving force to get back in control."

When James announced his ambitious plans, most people wrote it off as impossible. One response from a friend summed up his chances of success: "I don't think I could get an ice-cream cone in 50 states in 50 days." But armed with a purpose and the internet, James began laying the plans to prove them wrong. "There are no Iron Mans during the week. I had to create all 50 courses online on Google Earth. It took two and a half years to cover every inch of every one of these courses." Before he took his first step, James had visualized his task from start to finish. "You've got to combine your vision with massive amounts of action and work. Once I did that, my vision was so strong; I crossed all 50 before starting. There was no doubt."

On June 6, 2015, at midnight, James started his first Iron Man in Hawaii so he could catch the last flight out to get to Alaska the next day. The race was on. Almost immediately, however, the difficulty of what he was trying to do began to cloud his vision. "Days three and four were difficult because the excitement is gone, the adrenaline's gone, and the reality is setting in of what I committed to." The first week was rife with an internal struggle not to give up. "The longer you're out there, the more bored you get, and the more susceptible you become to getting talked out of what you're trying to achieve."

As the Road of Trials stretched on, James leaned on his training and an incredible team as he moved closer to the impossible. The Groundhog Day nature of the 50/50 was a blessing and a curse. He knew what he had to do; the challenge was staying focused long enough to get it done. "When things become the toughest, they should become the easiest, because you've mastered those basics. When you're in it and it's a fight, it's got to be automatic. Monotony is an underrated superpower." When the next step became a struggle, James had two wingmen (a schoolteacher on summer vacation and a friend who quit his job) to help propel him. "It was exactly what I needed. These two guys went all in. They understood what it meant to not make excuses and show up every day and grind. It was an unbelievable team."

The daily grind of racing was monotonous, but it was also full of surprises. The team chased a hurricane for three days, they hit a deer in the middle of the night between day six and seven, and the generator that provided the needed AC and refrigeration for their food decided it wasn't up for fifty days of work. "There's no perfect plan. At some point in time, you've got to run with it and figure it out along the way. I've seen so many people be too rigid and too dead set on their plan. I could be planning the 50 still today, trying to get it right." James credits his wife, Sunny, for making sure all the hiccups didn't turn into disasters. "When things would go south and I was consciously unconscious, she would step up to the table and say, 'This is what's going to happen. You are getting back on track. You are doing this. We're doing this.' She pulled all the strings to make it all come together."

Even with his family and team at his side, James found himself alone on the road. Getting to the other side of the fifty took James to the brink, not only physically but mentally and spiritually as well. On an almost daily basis, James would have to enter **The Cave** and listen to the voices that played on repeat. "Fourteen hours a day for seven weeks of you and your thoughts. You find out who you are." Digging inside was the hardest work James had to do. "You're not born with it. I wasn't born with it. It's something you have to figure out." James pushed away the voices until the final showdown nearly ended his race.

With twenty Iron Mans still ahead of him, James sat down on the side of the road, physically exhausted, and had a complete "emotional and spiritual collapse." But it was in the darkest corner of his mind he finally found himself. He closed his eyes and asked, "Why are you here? You know who you are; you know who you want to be. What needs to take place?" That's when the persona of the Iron Cowboy was born. He let go of the pain and fear, put his trust in his crew, and went inward, "a rebirth on the thirtieth day." He ran his last twenty races faster than his first thirty.

The 50/50 culminated with a race in James's home state of

Utah (he even got to sleep in a non-moving bed that night). Thirty-five hundred people showed up to witness history in the making. James didn't limp across the finish line; he flew. "Those last three miles, we dipped under seven minutes. We shed everybody. Had my coach not been there in person, he said he wouldn't have believed it." A decade of sacrifice and monotony and going to uncomfortable places had forged the Iron Cowboy into a legend.

When James talks about his legacy, he says he doesn't want to be exalted; he wants to be an example of what is possible. His inspiration has reached well beyond his inner circle and has rippled out across the world. "One of the coolest things I get to experience now are the emails I get where someone is training for their first race. They say, 'What you did was unbelievable, and I pulled strength from that.'" James is using his platform to help people find their own Iron Cowboy, "open up their minds and allow inspiration or gut feeling to take them where they're supposed to go."

TRAIL MARKER #6

A GRAND PURPOSE ATTRACTS DEVOTED ALLIES

"Most people...are like a falling leaf that drifts and turns in the air, flutters, and falls to the ground. But a few others are like stars which travel one defined path: no wind reaches them, they have within themselves their guide and path."

—HERMAN HESSE, *SIDDHARTHA*

Attracting incredible Allies is more than waiting for them to knock on your door; you have to have a compelling story to draw them in. A good friend of mine, Ganes McCullough, calls this "going somewhere with purpose." James Lawrence certainly had a compelling goal, attempting what most thought was impossible. His commitment, preparation, and audacious plan pulled incredible Allies to his side (one person even quit their job to be there!).

I've had the privilege of being drawn to incredible purposes over the past few years. One in particular is a nonprofit called the Waterboys. Waterboys was established by 2018 NFL Man of the Year Chris Long, with the purpose of bringing life-sustaining drinking water to communities in need. Once a year, Green Beret and former Seattle Seahawk Nate Boyer and Chris Long, along with combat veterans and NFL alumni take on Africa's highest peak to raise money for Waterboys. "Each new Conquering Kili class accepts the challenge to embark for the summit, a walk that represents the miles many African women journey on a daily basis to fetch water for their families. While training for the climb, each team member works to raise funds and transform communities through the gift of clean water" [3].

Because of my support for the veterans nonprofit Warrior Rising (chapter 8), I had the privilege and honor to join the 2019 Conquering Kili class. I found myself shoulder to shoulder with Green Berets and NFL Pro Bowlers as we embarked on a six-day journey to the summit. I was absolutely thrilled with the opportunity as I'm always trying to surround myself with people who inspire me to be more and do more. What I wasn't prepared for was how my definition of "more" was about to be expanded.

One of the veterans in our group was a man named Phil Quintana, or "Q," as he liked to be called. Q lost his left leg as a result of injuries sustained during his 2005 deployment in Afghanistan. He has a prosthetic, but it has limited function and support. Q trained for six months to climb Kili at Adaptive Training, a facility in Texas run by the former NFL player David Vobora. Coming back from war was hard enough, but coming back "incomplete" meant several dark years for Q. He told me how he had overcome that darkness and was doing this climb for everyone who had helped him and those still in need of help. I felt completely inadequate about my own why for doing the event, but I knew one thing: Q was getting to the top, and I would do everything I could to help.

Kilimanjaro is over thirty miles of walking and hiking spread over five days. The first four days are a grind but aren't difficult if you're used to walking or hiking long distances. But these weren't normal days for Q. He rarely got any breaks, constantly having to pull himself up hills and over rock formations. The last day is the true challenge. You're going straight up, in freezing temperatures, in the dark, and you can hardly breathe. It's the reason 43 percent of people who attempt to summit Kili end up heading back down. All eight NFL players and all the former military guys all said the same thing: it's the hardest thing they've ever done.

As dawn broke, I could see Q at the front of the group setting our pace. He was exhausted and clearly ready to be done, yet he pushed on dragging his leg up the mountain. At one point, I looked up and saw him literally crawling on all fours because he couldn't stand anymore. We made it to Gilman's Point, the spot most consider to be the top of the mountain. Technically, you could say you climbed up the mountain if this is where you turned around, but it wasn't the highest point in Africa. Uhuru Peak was still ahead.

Our guides huddled trying to decide how to proceed. Q's training partner, Dave Vobora, walked up and gave him a huge hug. He looked him in the eye and said, "Bullshit man! You aren't done yet. You got this. I know you and I know you aren't done. We've got ninety minutes of hell ahead of us, but the peak is in sight and you and I are going there right now—together." Q said okay, and away we all went.

Those ninety minutes seemed like five hours. We were at 19,000 feet, and the very serious issue of altitude was in full effect. Some of the toughest men I've ever met were in so much pain that they were struggling to get to the peak and stay for a few minutes so they could head back down. But they weren't going to let Q down. Q made the last steps to the summit with the help of his friends and guides, but we made it there because of him.

On the way down, I told Dave how inspiring his speech was. He said something I'll never forget: "We don't know how far we can truly go until we've pushed past where we've never been." He knew Q would look at every obstacle in his life differently for the next twenty years based on the decision he made in that moment. He knew Q could do it, and so he didn't hold back. That gift was given to all of us.

When you move with true purpose, you'll find yourself surrounded by people who will help you achieve the impossible.

HOW TO EXPLORE THE CAVE AND COME OUT BETTER

The process of creating an inner life that is congruent with your outer life may feel like a digression. Why go inside when you're charging hard on an outside path? Because it's the most direct route to what you ultimately seek—a more complete version of yourself.

You have to break yourself down to build yourself up in a new way. You can't reconfigure something that isn't in pieces. The Cave is the place where you ask the questions to pull apart the pieces. Where does it hurt? What am I hiding? Who do I want to be? When these questions destroy the armor you've been wearing and shatter what's underneath, you'll be able to kneel down and pick up only the pieces that matter. You venture into the dark to face those inner demons, to smash them, and let life come through.

GET TRACTION

1. **Be alone.** If you ask people what they are afraid of, they'll often say things like spiders, and heights, and death. Rarely will you hear a more common fear—being alone. Headphones and apps and drinks with friends are crammed into all the empty spaces of our lives. Whether conscious or unconscious, some of us ward off quiet like the plague. But that's where James Lawrence found himself, alone and bored for fifty days in a row. It was solitude that forced him into The Cave on his hands and knees so he could emerge renewed. Quiet the input and shut down the noise so you can finally hear the true heart beating inside you.

2. **Tell your truth unfiltered.** "I'm fine." If untrue, this small utterance creates the shaky foundation of your inner life. Brick by brick you'll add "all goods" and "I've got its" until it all comes crashing down. Sean Whalen's wall looked strong—money, house, cars—more than fine. Until it wasn't. Sean went into The Cave to tell the truth, to go to a place where no one else was looking, and to yell into the darkness that everything wasn't fine. And instead of feeling trapped by these truths, he felt free. He set down the rocks no one could see he was carrying and left them behind. When you open up to yourself and tell your truth unfiltered, the world gets lighter.

3. **Don't should all over yourself.** I shouldn't have a dark side. I shouldn't fail. I should be better. When you're inside The Cave, it's not about what you should find, but what's already there. Kyle Maynard had a list of shoulds in his life. He should feel thankful for what he has. He shouldn't feel sorry for himself. He should suck it up. But when he hit a bottom that couldn't be overcome by sheer will, he had to face the darkness. He had to go inside and see the shadow that existed in him and not run away. He had to accept that part of himself, whether anyone said he should or not. Leave the "I shoulds" at the mouth of The Cave and go looking for the "I ams."

4. **Isolation isn't preservation.** Many people avoid The Cave because they think they'll emerge in isolation; they'll have to admit to themselves, and to the world, they have a problem or desire unique to them alone. Baya Voce found the opposite to be true. When you feel ashamed by what you want or who you are, you aren't preserving

your place in society; you're closing yourself off from it. When you drag your desires out of The Cave and into the light, you find out you aren't the only one. There are other people who want to Explore with you if you tell them where you're headed.

Stepping out of The Cave, you'll finally feel whole. You overcame your most intimate test and gained the inner strength to match your outer toughness. You'll look up toward the next challenge with new eyes and a lighter pack. Your journey is reaching its peak. **The Mountain** looms.

CHAPTER 6

CLIMBING THE MOUNTAIN

"The one thing you can't take away from me is the way I choose to respond to what you do to me. The last of one's freedoms is to choose one's attitude in any given circumstance."

—VIKTOR FRANKL, *MAN'S SEARCH FOR MEANING*

Ever seen the movie *The Big Short*? The one tracking the financial crisis of 2007 triggered by the housing bubble? If you look closely in the background, you'll see me jumping on that bubble like a kid in a bouncy castle who doesn't know it's about to pop and trap him inside. I was all smiles and cotton candy. It never occurred to me there might be a limit to the fun.

The pre-crash real estate market was the party everyone was invited to. No guest list, no velvet rope. Money was being given away to anyone, no questions or employment verification asked. Want to buy a $250,000 house with no money down and no income? Why stop at one? Here's two. "Equity kings" were being crowned overnight. The unearned trophies were piling up on the shelves of speculators across the nation, and they couldn't (or didn't want to) see the whole thing was sagging under the weight. It wouldn't matter in the end. We all woke up one morning to the sound of someone ripping the shelf right off the wall. Everything fell.

I thought I was a real estate phenom. If I kept moving, no one would be able to catch me. That turned out to be true: no *one* caught me, but some *thing* did. I had the ego check of a lifetime. I wasn't a real estate wunderkind; I had the strongest tailwind in the history of real estate at my back. When it stopped, so did I. I went from selling ninety-eight homes a year to thirty. The average home price dropped 20 percent and with it my commissions. I was barely paying the bills.

I had to let my entire real estate team go except for my assistant who I cut to twenty hours a week. More often than not, I would give him his paycheck but tell him not to cash it until the next deal closed. Everyone I dealt with was in a desperate situation (myself included). I remember being at McDonald's with my sister and realizing I didn't have enough money to pay for my meal. She wrote an eight-dollar check to cover her big brother. I slouched down in my chair in disbelief at the heights I had fallen from.

The worst part was, nobody wanted to hear the truth. They were arranging deck chairs on this sinking ship to enhance its curb appeal. I met with a mailman who had purchased two investment properties for $600,000 each with nothing down. Now they were barely worth over $400,000. He couldn't understand how this was possible; it was a hole he refused to see he was in. I walked him outside and pointed down the street. Stuck in the freshly laid sod of every house on the block was the same sign—FOR SALE.

When I got knocked down by the crash, I picked up an acute case of Explorer's amnesia. I forgot all the lessons that got me where I was in the first place—I didn't seek help, I wasn't being honest about my struggles, and I was focusing on the pain and not the problem. For over a year, I was a Settler, hoping like hell someone would find me hiding in the corner and show me the way forward. **The Mountain** of rebuilding my business was blocking my path, and I didn't think I could climb it. I should have changed my voicemail to say, "Nobody came to see your home."

What saved me was the habit of work. The muscle memory I had built on my mission and the long days digging out of debt from the meat business. I never had to talk myself into going to work; it was like breathing to me—automatic.

I made over 5,800 calls that year to for-sale-by-owner listings. I listed 187 of those. I sold fifteen. Regardless of the outcome, I kept showing up as more and more Realtors were heading out the door. In less than two years, Utah went from over 6,000 agents to fewer than 1,400. The trail was getting less crowded, and my mindset began to shift. This collapse wasn't happening to me; it was happening *for* me. If I was willing to put in the work and see this cycle to the end, I knew it could be the defining point of my career.

Two years into the crisis, my moment finally came. When I was first starting out in real estate, a colleague of mine named Brad Lancaster was one of my key mentors. Not only was he the top agent in the office, but he had also been appointed to own and operate the first ever Keller Williams office in Utah County. When the market collapsed, the tables were suddenly turned. Brad made some questionable choices that not only pushed him out of Keller Williams but also lost him his real estate license, left him bankrupt, and got us both sued. If there was ever a time to cut ties with someone, this would be it.

Instead of pushing Brad out of my life, I made room for him. He'd lost a lot of my own money, but he hadn't lost my friendship. I gave Brad a job while he got back on his feet, and he eventually went out on his own buying homes at auction. The next time I heard from Brad, he wasn't looking for a favor. At the auctions, Brad met a buyer from a real estate investment trust in California. The buyer wanted to purchase hundreds of homes and was willing to come cash in hand for anything with four walls and a roof, and Brad wanted to bring me in on the deal. A possible "enemy" had become one of the strongest Allies for my business. My team sold eighty-five homes in three months, our most successful quarter to date. I made back five times what Brad had lost me in the crash. This was the turning point in my business and gave us the financial breathing room to reimagine our strategy. An unsuspecting Ally had pulled me to the summit.

The Mountain is the biggest outward test of the Explorer's journey. It's where you'll need all the tools and mental toughness at your disposal. All the rough roads you endured and hard-fought knowledge you earned will be needed for the climb. The next stories are of Explorers who faced monumental Mountains. Yet one foot in front of the other, they came out on top.

LIFE EXTENSIONS (LACY WEST)

Even at twelve years old, Lacy West knew she wasn't going to work in a conventional way. While most of her friends were earning money babysitting, Lacy had her mind in "entrepreneur mode." Lacy started a house-cleaning business with a selective clientele. "I only would clean houses of the old women in my neighborhood and from church because they weren't very messy." Lacy ran her business all through high school but still kept her eye on academics. She was taking advanced classes in law, preparing to be an attorney. But before graduating high school, Lacy won a pageant and was awarded a scholarship to a cosmetology school. Despite the teasing she received from family and friends, Lacy claimed her prize. "I thought having a hair license would be a great way to make money while I was in school, and cosmetology school was only one year."

What began as a slight detour before college turned out to be the Frontier that changed Lacy's life. "When I started hair school, I loved it so much I was like, yes, this is what I want to do." Lacy began her career assisting in a salon in Salt Lake City, but it wasn't long before she was looking for something bigger. "I always wanted to be in Vegas or Los Angeles. When I was visiting my family in Las Vegas, I applied at the Bellagio." Lacy didn't think she had a chance with such little experience, but at nineteen years old, she was offered the job and crossed The Bridge into the high-pressure world of entertainment. The biggest stars of the day from Paula Abdul to Muhammad Ali would take a seat in front of Lacy before they stepped onto the stage.

As her skill and knowledge of hair increased, Lacy's entrepreneurial mindset crept in again. "I wanted hair extensions for my own use, so I thought I would start my own company. I thought it'd be super easy." Her budding business, Lace Hair Extensions, caught on quickly as fellow hairstylists were drawn to the quality and color of the hair she was sourcing. But the long arm of law school finally caught up, not with her but with her husband who was accepted to the law program at Michigan. With the move and her second child on the way, Lacy's extension business slowed to a crawl.

Despite the diminished pace, Lacy was determined to stand on her own two feet. When her dad passed away when she was five years old, Lacy saw the hardships of a one-income family. "I saw my mom being a working single mother, and in the back of my mind I was always like, 'What if?'" Lacy began leveraging her network of celebrity stylists she met in Las Vegas, working late hours when her kids were asleep, and sending out samples for people to try. "When I had a good month, I saved the money and put it back into the business. I didn't go out and buy a new car or a new house." The investments paid off as orders were pouring in from around the country.

As the business was surging, Lacy's marriage was flagging. Her "what if" single-mom scenario was suddenly a "What now?" when her divorce was finalized. With sole custody of her two kids, Lacy knew the business had to continue to be successful. "My only choice was to make this work. I knew I would have to support my kids." With no financial backing and bad credit from a short sale of her house during the divorce, the success of her business was on her shoulders. Her mantra became, "I won't jump off that treadmill. I won't ever stop. So there's no way anyone can beat me."

While Lacy was running full steam ahead with her business, her body was putting on the brakes. "I was having insane migraines, I was having seizures, and everything pointed to a brain tumor." On Thanksgiving weekend, one of the busiest times for Lacy's online business, doctors confirmed she had a brain tumor in an inoperable spot. She was given a 20 percent chance of living if it were cancerous. The Mountain of Lacy's diagnosis stood ominously in front of her, but her climb was stalled as she waited to see if the tumor was growing. "That waiting game was probably the hardest thing I've ever gone through. Every month for six months, I was in and out of hospitals. They were poking me with crazy needles and giving me steroid treatments laced with a little bit of chemo to see what was going on." After six months of waiting, Lacy received two pieces of news. One, her tumor wasn't cancerous. Two, she was diagnosed with multiple sclerosis. It was the "best-worst news" Lacy had ever received. She had escaped a sure death sentence and was grateful to "only" have MS. "If I just would've had an MS diagnosis without the brain tumor part of it, I think I would have had a different attitude. I spent time in the neuroscience center and saw people literally dying right next to me. So I feel lucky every day. It's my second chance."

Lacy's time in the cancer center gave her a new outlook

on life and new focus for her passion of hair extensions. "I was in there and seeing all these women getting treated, and that's when it hit me: I have a way I can help people suffering from hair loss." During her treatment, Lacy had lost about 75 percent of her hair but was able to use her own products to remain confident in her appearance. But quality hair extensions are expensive, and she knew most people couldn't afford them on top of their medical bills. To help ease the emotional burden of hair loss, Lacy created the Lace Hair Foundation. "You can lose your hair for so many reasons. We're not limiting it to only cancer patients or only women going through trials. Any woman suffering from hair loss can apply." There are days when Lacy's MS prevents her from walking or seeing clearly, but her heart is always full of love. Every day she steps foot into her salon or works on the foundation is an opportunity to make a difference. "I love making women feel confident and beautiful. I believe there's a point people go overboard with being vain, but I also don't think there's anything wrong with feeling beautiful and confident."

A WARM PLACE TO PLAY (KYLE VAN NOY)

The one thing Kyle Van Noy wanted entering the NFL draft was a warm place to play. He ended up in Detroit. It wasn't warm, but at least the Lions played in a dome, and Kyle was happy to be making money. He'd reached the highest level of professional football, persevering through an up-and-down college football career at BYU. Kyle thought the hard part was over, but his new Frontier had another rocky road ahead. During his first real workouts with the team, he suffered an injury. The training staff didn't believe him and cleared him to keep playing. He took it easy during the summer, but Kyle knew something wasn't right when he returned for fall training camp. In a preseason game, Kyle made a routine tackle and went down with injuries the trainers couldn't ignore.

Kyle had barely crossed The Bridge into his pro career when an MRI revealed core muscle tears. "I ended up having five tears from one tear. Basically, my intestines were falling out." Kyle went through the first part of the surgery to fix the tears, sitting out the first eight games of the season and playing the remainder of the year with an untreated hip tear. Kyle finished the surgery in the off season, but the Lions pushed him through rehab before he felt ready to return. To add insult to injury, he had two bulging discs in his back and a pinched nerve in his left leg. The team was threatening to put him on the injured reserve list, which would have ended his season. "For the first time in my life, I was struggling to play the sport I love." The voice inside Kyle's head kept repeating, "I don't think I can do this. I can't play."

It would take a strong team of Allies around Kyle to lift him beyond his physical and mental hurdles. He found himself at the foot of **The Mountain** each morning when he got out of bed. "I hated going to work. I hated waking up and feeling helpless." But there were two people who didn't let Kyle throw in the towel—his trainer and his wife. Kyle refers to his wife as a "beast" in the most endearing way. "She would kick my ass to get up and go to work," not letting him wallow as he struggled. His trainer, Dave Daglow, was the "geeky, funky guy" who complemented the beast. He was a data-based trainer steering Kyle away from the traditional rehab workouts that were exacerbating his injuries. Before finding Daglow, Kyle battled with the Lions training staff on how to get him back on the field. "They had me doing stuff that wasn't helping. They basically didn't know what was wrong with me." Kyle says Daglow saved his career and gives him all the credit for why he stays healthy now. With his mental and physical games back on track, Kyle was getting more playing time and improving every day. Then another cold place came calling.

Kyle got the news he had been traded to the New England Patriots while he was at the hospital with his wife. For Kyle's wife, "it was the answer to her prayers," a release from the team and city that represented years of pain and struggle. Kyle didn't share the reaction. His first thought was, "Man, f*** Detroit for trading me." He was finally over the hump, playing well, gaining confidence, and enjoying the game again. Now he'd be joining a New England team already stacked with talent at his position. Kyle thought he had the summit of The Mountain in his sights, but it turned out to be a false peak. When he hung up the phone with Detroit's GM, he thought, "Cool, back to the bench I go."

Before he could get to the bench, Kyle had to get on a plane to Boston. On the same flight was former presidential candidate and current Utah senator Mitt Romney. Romney turned out to be a well-timed Guide as Kyle looked to turn his fortunes around. "Talking to him kind of gave me this new outlook on life. He had some ups and downs losing out on the presidency. It was cool getting another solid take from somebody like him, who doesn't give a damn about football. He's just a person who loves life and loves his family." Kyle arrived at his hotel at 1:00 a.m. and had to be at the Patriots practice facility at 5:00 a.m. He could barely keep his eyes open, but he was seeing with new clarity.

New England was definitely cold, but he got a warm reception in his new home. There was no official meeting when he landed in Foxborough, but the legendary coach Bill Belichick came up to him during a punt drill, looked him in the eye, and said, "I always get my guys." A handful of words was all it took for Kyle to feel like he belonged. "To have one of the greatest coaches in football say that to me, that gave me confidence. I'll always remember that." With a veteran defensive line in front of him, Kyle embraced his role as the "sixth man." He'd come off the bench late in games and even started a few games toward the end of the season as players got hurt. He was playing for the team, his personal injuries behind him.

The Patriots season went all the way to the Super Bowl where they recorded the largest comeback in history to defeat the Atlanta Falcons 34–28. In one year, Kyle had gone from almost quitting the game he loved to a Super Bowl champion. Yet, Kyle's Reward went well beyond the trophy. "It wasn't about me. It was about all the people who were behind me on my journey. I was playing with them on my shoulders and representing them." After a tough loss in the Super Bowl the following year, Kyle and the Patriots claimed another title in 2019. Kyle recorded a key defensive play that sealed the win.

TRAIL MARKER #7

A GUIDE IN WRECKER'S CLOTHING

When things are going poorly on your journey, you'll be convinced some-one or something is out to get you, a "wrecker" in your midst. Historically, a **Wrecker** was someone who would hang lights on cliffs as false bea-cons to lure ships into the rocks to crash and then steal their cargo from the wreckage. Although you'll want to blame your missteps and misfortunes on some outside force, on a Wrecker, it won't do you any good.

If you look hard enough, Wreckers are simply Guides, Allies, or Threshold Guardians you've mislabeled. I could have easily labeled my coworker Brad as a Wrecker. He lied to me, he lost my hard-earned money, and I would have been justified in shutting him out of my life. But in doing so, I would have missed a huge opportunity. By showing Brad love at his lowest point, he became an incredible Ally for my business. Friend or foe is merely up to the framing. An economic headwind for your business isn't a Wrecker; it's leading you toward a new path. A competitor who beats you in the race isn't a Wrecker; she's an Ally pushing you to be better.

When Kyle Van Noy first joined the Detroit Lions, he was convinced they were Wreckers. They weren't listening to him about his injuries and rushed him back on the field when he wasn't ready. Yet, the lesson he learned was about taking his health and recovery into his own hands. Their actions Guided him to a valuable piece of self-knowledge, which has propelled and prolonged his career.

Don't be a victim. Find the opportunity.

"Do I not destroy my enemies when I make them my friends?"

—ABRAHAM LINCOLN

NO SUMMIT OUT OF SIGHT (JORDAN ROMERO)

At nine years old, Jordan Romero's life was a lot more back and forth than forward progress. His parents were divorced, and he was splitting time between his mom's and dad's houses near Big Bear, California. He felt aimless. But at the beginning of fourth grade, Jordan was walking to class and a large mural caught his eye. "It was a colorful triangle within a triangle of the seven tallest summits in the world. I don't know why, but it fascinated me." Jordan finally had an anchor as he spent hours after school learning everything he could about climbing the world's tallest peaks—what gear you'd need, the right time of year to climb them, and which order to tackle them. He was obsessed.

After weeks of research, Jordan was ready to reveal his plan to his parents. He went to his dad first, who had a background in multiday expedition racing. If anyone would understand this desire, it would be him. His dad didn't say no; he handed him a backpack. "We went on an hour hike. I remember being ten or fifteen minutes into it and thinking, 'I hate this.'" He'd barely made it out of his own backyard, and he was ready to head back. But Jordan's dad, and Guide, wasn't going to let him turn around on his dream so easily. A few more practice runs and Jordan started to get into the flow of hiking and embraced the hardships of a climb. "It took a while to develop a passion for hiking because there are long periods of cold and monotony. Eventually, it became a time when I could put away my phone and focus."

Jordan kept up his research on the seven summits, and along with his dad and stepmom, concluded Mount Kilimanjaro in Africa would be their first target. "It wasn't as easy as writing out a check and it would happen. We had to get creative." Jordan set up a lemonade stand outside a local mountain bike shop. Half the proceeds went to Hurricane Katrina relief and the other half would fund their journey. They landed in Africa in July 2006, and Jordan began his quest for the seven summits. "It was at the summit that I was like, all right, one down, six to go. Let's go ahead and do them all." Jordan had Crossed the Bridge into professional mountaineering and wasn't looking back.

Yet, the path to become the youngest person to scale the seven summits was anything but smooth. Although Jordan and his family were able to cover some of their gear costs with sponsorships, the flights, permits, and guide costs piled up. They were scraping by to fulfill his dream. Nonetheless, he ticked off Mount Kosciuszko (7,310 ft) in Australia, Mount Elbrus (18,510 ft) in Russia, and Mount Aconcagua (22,841 ft) in Argentina, all in a single year. But Denali loomed in the distance. At 20,320 ft, Denali, North America's highest peak, wouldn't be the tallest he'd climbed, but it would be his most trying. With high avalanche danger and extreme weather swings, Denali was not to be taken lightly. "After Denali was done, I felt much more prepared to take on Everest."

Two years later, Jordan, his dad, and his stepmom were standing in front of the 2,000 pounds of gear they would need to scale the tallest point on the planet. Trying to block their path were the Threshold Guardians of a media firestorm. "They thought it was reckless for my dad and Karen [his stepmom] to let a thirteen-year-old take this on." But the team easily sidestepped these Guardians, knowing the preparation they'd done. "My dad was a lifeline paramedic and specialized in high-altitude medicine as well. It's not a reckless choice; it's about managing the problems and being able to mitigate them as you go along. If anything, we overdid it. Every couple of days, we would check in with each other. We were always on top of it."

If altitude wasn't an issue, it would take a relatively fit climber only seven or eight days from the base camp of Everest to the summit. But at the top of the world, Jordan's journey was going to take seven weeks. "If you go up too high too fast, you're going to die. When you're up at that high of altitude, you have to focus on being a human being. You have to drink an incredible amount of water every day."

No amount of preparation could shield the team from every danger of The Mountain. As the team was traversing the North Gulf, a saddle between Everest and a neighboring peak, disaster struck. "It's the only section of the climb there's glacier travel, and it was really warm that day. We get to this sketchy zone with a massive glacier shelf that often tends to collapse. My dad at one point said, 'Guys, we should pick up the pace. I don't have a good feeling about this.'" As they cleared the shelf, they passed two other climbers headed the other way. "Moments after we passed, it was so quiet and peaceful, and then all of a sudden there was a massive boom. I looked up, and there were ice chunks a hundred times the size of me coming down, turning into a slide. It definitely crossed my mind this was possibly my last day." The team survived, but not without a nasty cut on Jordan's dad's head from where he was struck by razor-sharp crampons. The two climbers they passed weren't so fortunate. "That was surreal for me to experience, especially being thirteen."

At 10:00 a.m. on May 22, 2010, thirteen-year-old Jordan became the youngest climber in history to summit Mount Everest (29,029 ft). But the record meant less to Jordan than the Reward of being there with people he cared about. "It was an emotional moment that brought our family so close together." Jordan's mom, who had been supporting him from afar, following his journey online from his GPS tracker, received a once-in-a-lifetime call from Jordan. "I said, 'Mom, it's your son, calling from the top of the world.'"

After conquering Mount Vinson (16,050 ft) in Antarctica the following year, Jordan had checked off all the seven summits and was ready to head back to level ground. "I've always been able to kind of blend in with my friends, but when I got back from Everest and then Vinson, it was hard to relate to them. I had seen so much that it was hard to describe to my peers." To work through what he'd experienced and also make his story more accessible to other Explorers, Jordan wrote a memoir, *No Summit Out of Sight: The True Story of the Youngest Person to Climb the Seven Summits*. In addition to the book, Jordan is a sought-after speaker at schools across the country. "I don't encourage kids to specifically climb Everest, but I tell them to be clear on what they want to do, be authentic to yourself, and do something that means a lot to you. This will put you on track to a fulfilling life."

RADICAL ACCEPTANCE (HAL ELROD)

Hal Elrod has died. Not a metaphorical death—it was clinical. A year before his brush with the other side, a twenty-year-old Hal was on top of the world as a record-breaking CutCo knife salesman. Hal was recruited to CutCo when he was in college and, in his first ten days, sold more knives than any other new hire in the fifty-year history of the company. His success wasn't a fluke and resulted in Hal becoming a recurring speaker at regional and national conferences. Returning home from a conference one night, he was reveling in his performance at the wheel of his shiny new Mustang. "I was getting on the freeway, and I was on cloud nine. I had gotten my first standing ovation. I felt on top of the world. I had no way of knowing my world was going to end." Seconds later, Hal was hit head-on by a drunk driver at seventy miles per hour. He was spun into another car that slammed into Hal's driver's side and crushed him inside. It took the paramedics an hour to pry him from the car with the Jaws of Life. "I broke eleven bones, I ruptured my spleen, I punctured my lung, I suffered permanent brain damage, and I began bleeding. I lost so much blood I technically bled to death. I was clinically dead for six minutes." After spending six days in a coma, Hal's ordeal was punctuated with the diagnosis he'd never walk again.

As he was lying in his hospital bed, Hal recalled a CutCo training about the five-minute rule. "When something goes wrong, according to your expectations, you set your timer for five minutes to bitch, moan, complain, cry, vent, whatever you gotta do. Feel the pain. When the timer goes off after five minutes, you acknowledge, I can't change what happened and there's no value in wishing I could." Instead of applauding his resilience, his doctors diagnosed him as depressed and delusional and encouraged Hal's parents to help him see reality. But Hal had already mentally moved into a new Frontier and the Threshold Guardians of the medical world weren't going to turn him back. He convinced his parents he wasn't crazy; he was simply committed. "I've accepted the worst-case scenario if I never walk again. I'll be the happiest person you ever see in a wheelchair. I promise you. I visualize that. I will not let it have power over my quality of life as I'm recovering. I can focus positively on the recovery instead of feeling sorry for myself."

Hal's commitment to recovery pushed him out of the wheelchair, but it wasn't the last time he'd get knocked down. When the economy crashed in 2008, Hal's fledgling coaching and speaking career took a huge hit as he lost half of his clients. The same man who had come back from the dead and defied doctors found himself in a six-month downward spiral he couldn't pull out of. "I couldn't pay my mortgage, I lost my house, my wife was pregnant, we had to move in with my dad, and I was $52,000 in credit card debt. I went into a real depression." **The Mountain** in front of Hal felt more daunting than the last. He had a family counting on him and a global economy stacked against him. Again, Hal reached back to lessons he'd learned at CutCo and knew change was within his control. There were other people in the world still enjoying success, and Hal was determined to figure out what they were doing differently.

As with many recent Explorers, Hal started with a Google search. No matter the keyword combination for "successful people," he kept landing on articles about morning rituals and routines. Hal was decidedly not a morning person. "I kept skipping them. Nope. Not doing that. Not happening. Where are the night owls who wake up late and are still successful?" But the trend was undeniable, and Hal came around to the (morning) light. "I backed my browser to the first one [article], read the first one, read the second one, read the third one, read the fourth one, and it totally shifted my perspective. I thought, 'Wait a minute. How you start your day is arguably the single most determining factor in your personal and professional success, because how you start the day sets the context and the tone for how you live your day and therefore your life." Hal's current morning routine consisted of setting the alarm clock for the last possible second he could wake up without losing his job and having his kids taken away from him. He had a tough climb ahead.

Hal narrowed down successful morning routines to six common habits: meditation, affirmations, visualization, exercise, reading, and journaling. Desperate for change, he didn't pick one or two; he did them all. Within a matter of days, Hal's depression lifted. His mind felt clear, his body felt stronger, and his confidence returned. "It happened so fast, it felt like a miracle. I started calling it my miracle morning. If I start every day this way, it's only a matter of time before my outer world begins to reflect my inner world."

Within two months of the "Miracle Morning," Hal had doubled his income, was in the best shape of his life, and was training for a fifty-two-mile ultramarathon (he'd never run before that). "When you dedicate the first part of your day to personal development, that's how you become the person who has the knowledge, the talent, the skills, the habits, and the mindset to create anything and everything you want for your life." The Miracle Morning was so effective that Hal wanted to share it with the few coaching clients who had stuck with him through the downturn. To make the morning routine easier to remember, Hal changed meditation to "silence" and journaling to "scribing," and the SAVERS acronym was born. Even though his clients were skeptical, "non-morning people" like Hal, they gave it a try. "Almost every one of them would come back to me and say, 'Hal, I had the best week in my sales career.'" Hal had guided himself and his clients from a mediocre morning to waking up better.

Almost a decade later, spreading the practice of the Miracle Morning still gets Hal out of bed without an alarm clock. Even though the SAVERS habits are ancient routines, he still sees them misinterpreted. "Affirmations have been taught wrong, in my opinion, for I don't know how long. Decades, centuries." Hal says we've been led astray by modern gurus who use affirmations in a fantasy way. "I am a millionaire. I am the most successful. It's these 'I am' statements that are based on things that aren't yet true. When we state affirmations that way, our subconscious calls bull****. It doesn't resonate as authentic." An even more harmful practice, according to Hal, is passive affirmations. "An example of a popular money affirmation is, 'Money flows to me effortlessly and in abundance.' No, it doesn't. That's not how money works. You usually have to work hard, create value to the world, and then you'll get paid for whatever value you have created."

Hal wants people to get real, get committed, and take action.

"We don't get what we want. We get what we're committed to. So if you want to be a millionaire, commit. Write it in the form of 'I am committed to becoming a millionaire.' That's very different." It's not a miracle; it's the way of the world. "When you create affirmations in that way, they're rooted in truth, they're supported by a deep meaningful why, they are supported and clarified with the actions necessary to achieving the results, and then you get specific as to when you are committed to taking those actions."

HOW TO REACH THE SUMMIT

Everything you learned along the way is put to the test on The Mountain. The small hurdles you faced on the Road of Trials will give you strength. The introspection you endured in The Cave will give you unwavering self-confidence. And with each obstacle you pass, you'll thank your past self for putting in the work. The less prepared will fall behind and drop out as you forge ahead to the top.

Whether it's a sizable debt, a challenging health issue, or rebuilding your identity from the ground up, The Mountain is the thing standing between you and the Reward you've been seeking. The final climb is what separates the committed Explorer from the half-hearted wanderer.

GET TRACTION

1. **Commit to making it to the top before you start.** There's a big difference between "I'm going to try to climb this mountain" and "I'm committed to climbing this mountain." The former has an easy out and a low threshold of success: "I made it only halfway, but I tried." When you're standing at the foot of The Mountain, don't make an attempt; make a commitment like Hal Elrod or Jordan Romero.

2. **Take the switchbacks.** Have you ever seen a trail going in a straight line from the bottom of a huge mountain to the top? Of course not. It would be prohibitively steep to head straight up, so switchbacks are used to smooth the ascent. Kyle Van Noy's football career was a series of switchbacks before he made it to the top. His slow ascent through different coaches and teams and injuries put him at the summit at the pace he needed. As you're slowly working your way through the switchbacks of your own climb, don't be swayed by the illusion of the straight path up.

3. **Get clarity on the climb.** Most of the climb up a mountain is monotony. But the hours between the trailhead and the summit can be some of the most useful of your journey. When Lacy West was trekking up The Mountain of her brain tumor recovery, she had months in the cancer center to take stock of her life and her business. It was in these focused, uphill moments that the purpose of her business expanded. Don't wallow in the wasted hours up The Mountain. The climb is where you'll get even more clarity on the purpose of your journey.

You made it. You're up among the clouds and proved all the naysayers wrong. With your flag firmly planted, you breathe out and look down at the treasure chest at your feet. It's time to claim your **Reward**.

CHAPTER 7

UNCOVERING THE REWARD

"A man who finds no satisfaction in himself will seek for it in vain elsewhere."

—FRANÇOIS DE LA ROCHEFOUCAULD

As a single guy around the holidays, I always felt more sorry for myself than grateful. After several years of wallowing in my loneliness, I decided to force myself back into the giving spirit by raising money for Sub for Santa. I couldn't free my mind completely from my solo predicament because the only fundraiser idea I could come up with was a date auction. I enlisted my most generous single friends to step up and help meet the goal of raising enough money to fund Christmas for three or four families.

Even though we were in a down economy, I was blown

away by people's willingness to give. We raised $32,000 at the auction, an amount that would support 200 more kids than planned. I spent all of December researching the families, understanding what they needed and getting all the details right. Over seventy people volunteered to help buy, wrap, and deliver the presents. After a two-week push, I was exhausted but incredibly happy with what we were able to provide those families.

I woke up on Christmas Eve expecting a leisurely day with family but instead received a frantic phone call. One of the people who submitted a name of a family said she hadn't heard from me and no gifts had been delivered. I quickly went back through my emails and couldn't find anything about this family. All of the gifts had been delivered, and there wasn't any more money. I tried to roll over and go back to sleep. I'd done what I could, and I didn't feel like dealing with someone else's oversight. But that little voice connecting our heads to our hearts wouldn't leave me alone, and this quote kept rolling through my mind: "You will never regret blessing someone else's life."

I rushed out to buy the gifts and threw them in big garbage sacks with rolls of wrapping paper. I called the family from the road and told them I'd be there by 10:00 p.m. It turns out they were a Spanish-speaking family, and I thanked my past self for Crossing the Bridge on my mission to Mexico. As I started to drive, a mini Road of Trials unfolded before me. The sky opened up into a massive blizzard, and my GPS took me to a roundabout in the middle of nowhere. There were no houses in sight. It was 10:15 p.m. on Christmas Eve, and I was alone (again) and lost. I was about to leave when I saw a dim light flickering in the window of a barely visible house out in a field.

With three bags full of toys, I trudged through the snow, pushing through my growing annoyance. The parents answered the door and whispered the kids were asleep. Once inside, I could see a sparsely decorated tree and not one gift underneath it. The rest of the house was just as bare. As I unloaded the gifts and handed them the wrapping paper, they broke down crying. The guilt and anguish of their kids almost waking up to an empty tree came pouring out. I couldn't help but join in, my own selfishness falling away with the tears.

As I got up to leave, the mother let go of her husband's hand and rushed toward the stove. She picked up their only hot pad and pressed it into my hands. I tried to decline like I did with the TV remote they offered when I arrived, but she insisted. I graciously accepted it and ducked out the door. I didn't trudge on the way back to my car, and I definitely didn't feel alone. What I thought was going to be the inconvenience of my Christmas became the best Christmas of my life and a **Reward** I'll never forget.

Like me, this next set of Explorers had different outcomes

in mind when they embarked on their journeys. For one, it was the riches and fame of a career in the NBA and for another, the easy joys of being a new parent. Yet, the curves in their paths found them off the course they had predicted. And with unexpected ends came unexpected Rewards.

UP SYNDROME (OAKLEY PETERSON)

Oakley Peterson had the perfect pregnancy. There was nothing abnormal in her blood work, and the ultrasounds didn't raise any eyebrows. "We had no indications we were going to have a child that was any different than our first." When the baby was born, Oakley thought he was a little "shorter and stubbier" than her daughter, but the doctors and nurses knew it was more than that. Oakley and her husband, Scott, were annoyed but relented when they requested to run a few tests. "I wasn't even worried for the first few minutes. They're going to take him and realize they worried us for nothing. As soon as I saw Scott walking back down the hall, it was all over his face. My whole world crashed."

Oakley's new baby, Wells, had Down syndrome. "Immediately, you start jumping from being in the hospital to what they're going to look like at twenty years old. They're never getting married; they're never going to have kids. I thought I had all these answers and I knew nothing about Down syndrome." The hospital didn't help dispel her fears, overwhelming Oakley and Scott with piles of literature she only later realized were outdated. "Chances of leukemia, chances of a dual diagnosis with autism, chances of celiac disease, all the possibilities. What if other parents had a website telling them about all the chances of their kids abusing drugs, chances of getting knocked up in high school, chances of run-ins with the law. Would we still want to have kids?"

The Charted Territory of forty-six chromosomes was gone, and the Frontier of forty-seven had arrived. "For nine months, you dream up this baby. I had already decorated a nursery, and I had to return everything because it felt like that kid was gone. I had to say goodbye to what I thought I was having before I could fully embrace what I had." Wells wasn't the baby Oakley and Scott expected, but he was the baby they needed. "I remember holding him in the NICU and looking in his eyes and thinking, 'Wow, this kid has so much wisdom in these little newborn eyes.'"

Instead of life crashing down, Wells brought everyone up. "I always call it Up syndrome because it elevates us; we love it." And it wasn't just with family. Wells left a trail of smiles wherever he went; the bus driver, the cashier at the grocery store, no one was immune. "He's a little ray of light; he exudes pure joy." Even on the hard days, Oakley says Wells has made her life easier by resetting her expectations. "It was a huge refining moment in my life. I had to step back and evaluate what I wanted for my family and realized I could still have that with this child. I want my children to be good, kind humans who are doing good things in society and are making a difference in the world around them. Done. Check. Wells was born that way and he is that way."

Oakley's enduring **Rewards** have been the daily lessons she learns from Wells. "He teaches. He teaches us to step back and enjoy the little things." The magic of an extra chromosome has improved all the relationships in Oakley's life. "One of the greatest lessons he's taught me, because my firstborn can be quite challenging in her own ways, is to step back and let her be her. Stop trying to make her who I feel she should be or fit her into what other kids her age are doing. Wells has taught me to stop, drop the expectations, and let her figure it out." A Harvard study backs this up [1]. Researchers found families who have a child with Down syndrome were happier and had better relationships with their siblings.

Having struggled without guidance in the beginning, Oakley wanted to provide an alternative to the hospital literature. Her blog, *Nothing Down about It*, aims to dispel the fear and negativity for new parents and shows the full and rich life that is possible for a family with a Down syndrome child. "I always say, every child has special needs, and my son's special needs are more obvious than your child's special needs. But I wanted people to read our blog and say, 'Wow, that's a beautiful life. Down syndrome isn't holding them back.'" Oakley's outreach has had an unexpected impact overseas. "In some parts of the world, Down syndrome is still very taboo and not widely accepted. The rare people who decide to keep that child need so much support. We've been able to help people all over the world with those adjustment periods, and there's nothing more rewarding than that."

Oakley's life isn't what she expected. These weren't The Mountains she thought she would climb. But the Frontiers she's forged with Wells are where she's found freedom. "I tell people to stop trying to control life. Let it surprise you; let things come. And usually, those surprises end up being the best things that happen to us."

TREASURES OF THE EAST (JIMMER FREDETTE)

"Do you guys play with three-pointers?" That's the question Jimmer Fredette's dad would have to ask before his six-year-old stepped onto the basketball court. The opposing coaches and referees hadn't even considered it, as most kids couldn't hit the rim from the three-point line, let alone make them. But Jimmer could. "I had a mindset I could make any shot. You have to have that type of mentality if you want to be a great basketball player. I believed I was the best one on the court whenever I was out there, and that gives you the confidence to go do what you want to do."

From six years old through his senior season at BYU, Jimmer was always the best player on the court. He had the scoring records and trophies to back it up, and he had BYU ranked in the top ten for the first time in over twenty years. After a signature win over another top-ranked team, San Diego State, Jimmer was thrust into the national limelight. "I literally couldn't get to my class the next day. People were coming up and coming up asking for pictures and autographs, and I missed the whole class." Jimmer's prolific shooting and BYU's deep playoff run gripped the college basketball world. And although he fell short of capturing a national championship for the Cougars, Jimmer was unanimously named the national college player of the year and won the ESPY Award for Best Male College Athlete. Jimmer was projected to be a top-fifteen pick in the NBA draft and continue to excel on basketball's biggest stage.

Selected as the tenth pick in the NBA draft, Jimmer landed with the Sacramento Kings. The wildfire of "Jimmer Mania" spread to the NBA and his number seven jersey instantly sold out. If only merchandise equated to playing time. Five games into his rookie season, Paul Westfall, the coach and Guide who had lobbied to bring Jimmer to the Kings, was fired. "Paul was the one who loved me, and I was doing well. Then all of a sudden, he gets fired, and things change in a heartbeat. I went from playing a lot to all of a sudden hardly playing at all. Some games I'd play two minutes and come out; some games I'd play eighteen minutes. It was inconsistent and kind of all over the map." The confidence that carried him to the heights of his career suddenly evaporated. He had crossed The Bridge into professional basketball, and it felt anything but familiar. "It was something I had never dealt with before. What am I doing wrong? Am I not good anymore?"

The people who should have been Jimmer's strongest Allies turned into unsuspecting adversaries. The owners of the Kings were trying to sell the team and became very hands off. The lack of leadership permeated the organization from top to bottom, everyone trying to save their own jobs instead of working as a team. "In the locker room, it was hard to control guys. Guys were playing for themselves, and I'll put myself in that boat. Everyone was trying to be like, 'Hey, I can still play.' It wasn't a true team; it was more like whoever caught it was going to shoot the basketball." Jimmer's moment in the NBA seemed to be slipping away, and his fans weren't helping his cause. "If I wasn't playing, the coaches would get yelled at, and it was awkward for me. I didn't like it because I knew some of the coaches were like, 'I don't want to put him in because these guys are telling me to.'" Jimmer's Road of Trials through the NBA ended after five seasons and four different teams. "I don't know 100 percent why I didn't play, but it was difficult. It was very, very tough for me."

In 2016, a new Frontier opened up for Jimmer when he signed with the Shanghai Sharks of the Chinese Basketball

Association (CBA). He went around the Threshold Guardians of the NBA to get back on a professional court, and he returned with force. In one of his first games of the season, Jimmer scored fifty-one points in front of an electrified crowd. He added an incredible seventy-three-point performance a few months later. "Jimmer Mania" headed east as he was named the CBA's Regular Season MVP. "Being able to go to the Chinese basketball league has been a huge part of my career. It helped me become a better basketball player and succeed even more than I thought I could in the NBA. I was able to get my confidence back. I've been able to find myself again, being able to play my game of basketball and show people what I can do."

The basketball world beyond the NBA also expanded the scope of Jimmer's **Rewards**. The CBA is the second highest paying league in the world behind the NBA, coupled with one of the shortest seasons. "I'm making more money in China now than I would have made in the NBA. It's lucrative, and I get to play my style of basketball." To top it off, unlike the NBA where only a handful of the league's superstars get the lion's share of sponsorship deals, Jimmer has plenty of opportunities off the court in China. "My shoe product is probably my favorite. That's been super cool. They've made two signature shoes for me so far, and next year they're going to make it three."

Even though Jimmer would love to get back to the NBA,

he's keeping his options open, knowing there's more than one path to success. "I don't care about the narrative at this point. I'm more concerned about providing for my family and making sure we're secure while also making sure I'm having fun playing basketball."

PUTTING FOOD ON THE TABLE (ANDREW SMITH)

In the late '90s, Andrew Smith had visions of becoming the next tech billionaire. The media streaming company he had started with a couple of roommates was on the verge of a massive IPO. "We were having a lot of success. Where others didn't have revenue, we had revenue. We were thinking about going public, and then the market popped." When the tech bubble burst, several zeros were shaved off his company's valuation. "I believe there was a higher power somewhere in the universe that thought if I give Andrew one hundred million dollars today, I'm probably going to ruin that dude."

Andrew got a smaller (but lucrative) payout when he sold his company a few years later. But **The Reward** he didn't expect was learning how to survive and thrive in down markets. "What I learned was far beyond what I thought I could have made. You go through a bubble burst in the market, when the market retracts as hard as it did in 2000 and 2001, as a CEO and I'm telling you right now, you grow some hair on every part of your body you didn't think you had before. It's difficult; it's trying times."

The market wasn't through providing Andrew with tough lessons. His next venture, a software company that built inventory tracking for homebuilders, was a victim of the housing market crash in 2008. Any business related to housing was tightening their belts, and "nice to have" software was usually the first to go. Andrew saw a 60 percent drop in customers almost overnight. Instead of trying to plow headfirst into the Threshold Guardian of market pressure, Andrew went around it. "We had a proven model, a proven business, so I immediately jumped on a plane and went north. Canada wasn't hit like we were, so I decided to live there and try to get new markets to open up."

Having already been through one market collapse, Andrew knew how to weather the storm. Instead of panicking, he asked himself questions. "What am I being told to learn here? Why am I going through this? I've seen this movie before; I experienced this movie a couple years ago and I know how it ends. I see the credits coming. Let's change the ending." Andrew led his team through his second Road of Trials, sold the company for a healthy profit, and went looking for a challenging new Frontier.

In an unlikely move for a tech CEO, Andrew set out to explore the restaurant business. When he crossed The Bridge into the world of restaurateur, he knew only two things: the food industry was uncorrelated to market shifts (he'd had enough of that), and he wanted to take the

Rewards of entrepreneurship to a wider audience. Andrew was willing to explore the areas of the food industry most people took for granted. "I wanted to prove it's not such a risky market even though the failure rate is 80 percent." As someone with fresh eyes, he was able to find the inefficiencies. "Most restaurateurs focus on the restaurant, customer experience, and food, and they don't focus on the other stuff. They go home at night and push all the bills, the HR issues, and facility management to the corner of their desk. I could come in and professionalize that and make better money at the restaurant level. I could also make it so the dream of restaurant ownership, which is not attainable for most people, would be attainable."

Andrew built his restaurant business, Four Foods Group (Kneaders Bakery & Café, Little Caesars Pizza, Swig, and more) on the foundation of shared success. When Four Foods acquires a new brand, they're looking for a partnership, not a buyout. "We don't want the founders to disappear. We buy in half of the company, and when we give the founders that check, we want them to put it away and then we want them to focus on the business with us." Andrew revels in seeing his employees and partners reap the Rewards of their hard work. "It's no fun to take a pile and push it into your own satchel. It feels good to cut checks out to everybody. I love walking up to people and saying, 'Here's your check for the quarter.' To see their eyes and hear them say, 'This is a game changer for me,' that's what drives me."

Ultimately, Andrew is focused on opening new Frontiers to as many people as he can reach. Not only is he interested in building careers for his more than 5,000 employees and partners, but he also wants to lift the industry as a whole. "We don't hold our cards super tight; we open up and say, this is what we're doing. This is how we're performing, this is what sites are good, these are the vendors we're using, and this is how we've saved our money. We share data because we're all trying to help each other." Andrew bases his success on the bottom line of people, not profits. "Over the last eleven years, we've created 16,500 jobs. We're teaching skillsets these kids will use forever. My main drive right now is creating opportunity for others and making it so they can win in their careers and their life. If you're focused on the dollars and cents and how that gets into your pocket faster, it's a hollow path because once you get there, it's so anticlimactic."

TRAIL MARKER #8

FILL THE JAR TO RETAIN YOUR ALLIES

You attract Allies with vision, but you keep them with trust. You create trust through consistency. Brené Brown, a courage and vulnerability researcher at the University of Houston, refers to the moments where trust is created or destroyed as "marble jar moments" [1]. Every relationship you have with someone comes with a jar. You can either deposit a marble into the jar with kindness and generosity or take one out when you don't show up. It's easy to attract Allies with a flashy vision, but it's much harder to show up every day and fill the jar to keep them by your side. Andrew Smith understands the power of this consistency and makes a point to fill the jars of his employees, partners, and competitors. His business isn't built on the backs of others but on the foundation of trust.

Building trust with my Allies has always been a core tenet of who I am. As an Explorer and risk taker, I need to know I can trust the people around me and vice versa. Trust always pays off in the end, and I can prove it. In 2014, Trevor Milton (chapter 2) confided in me about his idea for Nikola Motors. He told me point blank, "I know how to do this, it's a billion-dollar idea, and it will work. But it will cost me five years of my life." When he showed me the concept, not only did I encourage him to go for it; I also begged him to let me invest. Eventually, he let me give him all the money I had to my name. I even sold off a few real estate properties and invested all of those profits as well. I was one of the handful of noninstitutional investors he brought in early. And as of the writing of this book, Nikola turned out to be more than a billion-dollar idea; it was a $22 billion idea and counting. But why did he let me in? Because I've been filling the jar of our friendship for over a decade.

The first marble that went in the jar was on Trevor's birthday in 2015. Trevor had sold his company dHybrid Systems for a huge profit and wanted to celebrate big for his birthday. He invited thirty people on an all-expenses-paid trip to Hawaii. He rented an amazing beach house and fleet of SUVs to take us on excursions around the island. The first morning was going to be a hike, and it was nothing short of chaos getting thirty people ready and out the door for the hour drive. Everyone jumped in wherever there was space, and we took off on the hour ride to the trailhead.

We were thirty minutes into an amazing hike when someone said, "Where's Trevor?" It was a classic case of "I thought he was with you." Trevor was still at the house, and we were too far to go back and get him. Everyone tried frantically to get ahold of him, but he wasn't picking up his phone. It became clear his phone wasn't off when he sent a mass text, which roughly said, "I can't believe you left me on my birthday; you're all terrible. Enjoy the trip. I'm headed back to the airport." Inside of trying to apologize like everyone else, I sent him a Venmo payment for $4,000 and this message: "I don't need your money. I came here to celebrate with you and to get to know you better. I've had a similar experience if you want to call me back and talk about it." A few minutes later, my phone rang.

I told Trevor how my supposed best friends had also left me adrift (quite literally) at my own party as well. The previous summer, I had organized a houseboat trip on Lake Powell in Utah. We had already parked the houseboat in a canyon, but I had to take the ski boat back to the marina to pick up a group of people who had shown up late. But when I filled the boat with people, I forgot to fill up the tank. We were less than a mile from the houseboat when we ran out of gas. It was getting dark, but I wasn't worried as all of my best friends were on the trip, and I knew they'd eventually come looking for us. But they didn't. They left us there all night while they had a dance party, assuming we were fine. When they came and found us the next morning, I had a vision of burning the whole weekend down and telling everyone to piss off; I would have been justified. Instead, I took an hour to myself, chalked it up to an honest mistake, and enjoyed a fun weekend with friends.

When I shared my story, Trevor and I weren't that close. But by being vulnerable, by finding common ground, I was filling the jar. He came back to his party, and he's been one of my best friends ever since. We've each had moments where we filled the jar for each other, marble by marble, consistently creating our bond. So when I put my life savings into Nikola Motors and he accepted, it was far from speculation. Neither of us got lucky; we had trust.

THE REWARD YOU DIDN'T GO LOOKING FOR

It's been many years since my Sub for Santa date auction, but every Christmas Eve, I pull out my hot pad and put myself back in that little house. The lasting Reward of the Explorer is rarely what was initially sought. Organizing that fundraiser, I was seeking a sense of accomplishment, the feeling of doing something good, and hopefully, a sense of feeling less alone. What I ultimately found was a lesson in humility and gratitude I carry with me to this day.

Although the trophy, or the IPO, will initially drive you and sustain you through the rough patches, the lasting value of personal change will be the Reward that doesn't fade. Your heart will change, beating fast with excitement, not fear, as you cross future bridges. Your hands will change, gripping tightly to Allies and Guides when you're being pulled from your path. Your feet will change, the calluses of previous climbs protecting you on the next ascent. Your soul will change, filled by giving back to others, not taking for yourself. This process of personal alchemy is the true Reward, the one that can't be swept up once the ticker tape parade is over.

GET TRACTION

1. **Be open to life's surprise Rewards.** You don't always get what you want, but you often get what you need. It's a cliché at this point, but the core truth is hard to dispute. Oakley Peterson thought she knew what she wanted—a "normal" baby who would fit right into her "normal" world. What she got was an atypical baby who didn't fit into her world—he expanded it. Surprise Rewards are there if you're looking.

2. **Don't stop three feet short of gold.** There's a story made famous by Napoleon Hill about a Colorado gold miner. After several months of searching, he figured his claim was worthless and sold his plot and equipment to a local junk man. The new owner, with advice from an engineer, started digging three feet from where the first miner stopped. He struck gold. That story very likely could have been about Jimmer Fredette. He could have given up on basketball, given up on his claim. Instead, he moved three feet (and seven thousand miles) over and struck gold in China. Don't stop three feet short of your Reward. Keep digging.

3. **Extend the Reward by giving it away.** The positive bump of The Reward you worked so hard for on your journey will quickly fade if you don't use the Andrew Smith method—giving. When his company experiences success, he doesn't think about what it means for him but how much he can give to others. Another zero in your bank account will fade, but the feeling of making an impact in someone else's life has lasting power.

The Explorer's path isn't a line; it's a circle. It's time to make the trek back down and **Return** to where you started.

PHASE IV

TRANSMITTING YOUR SOUL

With the summit scaled, the treasure found, you'll linger at the top to take in the view. But the pull back home, back to the beginning of your journey, will sneak in and set you back down the path. This is **The Return**. As you pass familiar landmarks, you'll see them differently. You're not the same person who went up. But don't mistake downhill for easy. The world you left and the people who didn't come with you may initially balk at your change. Yet you'll move forward, whether your old world or old friends want to follow you or not.

As you inch closer to home, you'll recall all of the help you received along the way and know the last part of your journey must be a repayment of those favors. This is called **Filling In The Map**. You'll seek out a way to integrate what you've learned and how to share your wisdom with the world. You'll give freely and generously of the gifts you found, knowing there is an abundance up ahead.

CHAPTER 8

MAKING THE RETURN

"You cannot stay on the summit forever; you have to come down again. So why bother in the first place? Just this: What is above knows what is below, but what is below does not know what is above. One climbs, one sees. One descends, one sees no longer, but one has seen."

—RENÉ DAUMAL

I emerged from the real estate crash with my name head-lining a successful business. Not only was I the face, but I thought I was the arms, too, single-handedly holding up the roof. Our clients needed me to be visible at every step of the process, or things would come crashing down. It wasn't that I didn't trust and respect my team, but I had a role to play, and it felt like no one else could do it.

But as usually happens when you find yourself on a peak, I looked beyond and saw taller mountains in the distance. I had a vision of growing our business beyond residential real estate, so I applied and was accepted into a master's program at Arizona State. This meant the face of our business (mine) would need to be looking at a professor in another state and not at our clients. I had a choice to make: keep playing Atlas from afar and slow down our operation or allow the capable people on my team to shoulder the load.

I went with option B and spent the next year training and preparing my team for my absence. I showed them the techniques that made me successful and gave them the space to make it their own. But when I got on the plane to leave, I still wasn't convinced they could do it without me. I could already see the line of angry clients staring at my empty chair and demanding me back to close their deals.

The outcome wasn't even close to what I expected. The next year, without me constantly in the spotlight, we had our best year on record. The business didn't shrivel; it thrived. I was humbled like I've never been before. Coming off the top of The Mountain made space for my team to climb up. It allowed them to explore the Frontiers I'd already crossed and freed me to incorporate all the lessons and learnings from my first eight years in real estate. No longer tethered to the office, I could explore my passion for connecting and teaching without adversely impacting the business.

Because the Road of Trials is so arduous and climbing The

Mountain is such an accomplishment, it's hard to convince ourselves to come back down, to make **The Return**. The view from the top is not one we readily relinquish. Why leave for a startup when you've finally been made VP of marketing after fifteen years of slogging? Why start training for the next race when it feels so good to sit down and hold the trophy you won? Because staying on top is another form of settling. In the beginning of a journey, the comfort of your Charted Territory holds you back from pushing into the Frontier. At the end, the sweet taste of triumph can plant you right back on the couch of comfort. An Explorer doesn't feel bad about taking a breather at the top, but they understand new Frontiers aren't found sitting still.

The following Explorers are people who struggled to make The Return. They paced at the top afraid they'd never make it back to the same heights. But on the way back down, they discovered they had become more than their accomplishments.

THE GREATEST MINORITY (JOHN PESTANA)

John Pestana started as a music major in college and was working toward becoming a high school choir director. There was only one problem: a job as a choir director didn't pass his mother's "test." She had always told John he needed to find a career where he could make at least $200,000 a year. He's not sure where she got that number since both his parents combined never made over $80,000 a year, but nevertheless, her words stuck. Halfway through college, he switched from music to business and got to work making money as a computer lab manager.

John's interest in computers quickly filled the musical gaps, and he searched for ways to integrate technology into the business career he was driving toward. He stumbled onto the budding Frontier of the internet when a friend recommended him to a campus club. "It was really kind of a Unix users group slash internet club. I'd heard about the internet, but didn't know what it was. The very first day, I was intrigued by the whole concept. I asked them if I could join the club and be the president. They looked at me like I was crazy. 'Well, you can be the secretary, I guess.'" Two months later, John was the vice president and leading the charge to expand.

As the internet was based on a strong network of users, John knew the club needed more members. "We needed to figure out how to help spread the message of this internet thing." John volunteered to start website programming classes to pull people in. "I only held three of those meetings before I was too busy." Word spread of John's coding prowess, and he was approached by professors and small business owners to build them websites. "Back in those days, I priced it based off of how many pages you wanted; it was $300 a page. I started building websites for people and kept getting bigger and bigger projects." The following spring, John got married, and instead of unwrapping their wedding presents, they sold them. With the proceeds from their gifts and a small amount of savings, John and former classmate Josh James founded their first official website-building company.

Josh turned out to be a powerful Ally who complemented John's business and technology background with an eye for marketing and sales. The company attracted larger clients, but one in particular opened their eyes to the real opportunity in front of them. "We built a web page builder for this company, and I charged them $30,000 to build it. They sold their business for $10 million. We didn't make money unless I was programming a web page; I was trading dollars for hours. We were on the wrong side of the deal." The team began searching for something they could own, a way to "make money while they slept." After trying and failing at dozens of ideas, a friend approached the team with an idea for tracking visitors on a website. "We were already familiar with that because we used a program called Web Trends to track server logs. It was a horribly inefficient way to track a website. We ran with this idea of tracking with a tag, which is this little piece of JavaScript that gets embedded into your code." That little piece of JavaScript turned into a fast-growing business. John and Josh bought out the friend they had partnered with; they'd found their nighttime moneymaker.

As their business matured, John and Josh encountered the ups and downs of the Road of Trials. "We were young, we were excited. But there were times when we were laying on the floor crying wondering how in the heck we were going to keep things running." Both founders had to mortgage their houses to make payroll at one point. Yet, despite the near misses, the company was growing and had attracted an offer to be acquired. The team was on the verge of the lucrative buyout they'd been dreaming of. What they didn't see coming was the nightmare of the dot-com bubble. The bubble burst before the acquisition could be finalized. "We ended up letting go of a whole bunch of people a couple weeks before Christmas in 2001. We had no money to even do a severance or anything."

They were back at the bottom, but John and Josh kept their eyes looking up. They streamlined their business by selling off components and sharpened their focus as an enterprise data company. "We put down our heads and moved forward. That's when the lights came on. That's when Omniture came into existence. We changed the name of the company, and all of a sudden, we couldn't sign people up fast enough. We were growing over 100 percent every single year for over five years." Their growth culminated in an acquisition that didn't falter. Omniture was acquired by Adobe in 2009 for $1.8 billion. John had made his mother proud, easily clearing her $200,000 goalpost.

With his goal met, John found himself at the top with no new challenge on the horizon. Although he did feel a certain level of accomplishment for having "the biggest success in the history of Utah," the quiet whisper of "What's next?" kept ringing in his ears. "When you've had a lot of success, I'm talking emotionally now, all of a sudden you feel a little bit like Michael Jordan who's now starting to play baseball." John was a thirty-five-year-old who felt like he was starting over. **The Return** for John was a lot like the beginning of the journey, a jumble of fear and uncertainty. "Everybody wants you to hit a grand slam and you feel a lot of pressure. Can I do it? Can I hit another grand slam?" John knew second companies usually flopped and pressure in his personal life mounted as well. Overnight, John's entire life "became a business," and he had to hire staff to manage the day-to-day. John's path down The Mountain was even more complicated than going up.

The key to John's Return was shifting the focus from himself to putting his energy into making the entrepreneurial journey fair and equitable for others. He used his platform and resources to help clear the path of Threshold Guardians with the founding of the nonprofit Libertas Institute. Libertas supports a vision "for each Utahan to pursue a better life by removing obstacles that limit opportunity." John wants to level the playing field for everyone who wants to start a business. "Entrepreneurs and employees deserve fair competition and the elimination of unnecessary regulations. There are plenty of people here in this state who say they're freedom minded, but then they will oppress people by forcing stores to be closed on Sunday for Sabbath. What about the person who is a Seventh-Day Adventist? Their Sabbath is Saturday. If the state was 70 percent Seventh-Day Adventists, would we want them to oppress us? The most important person is the individual, and we have to protect the rights of the individual because that's the greatest minority, when it's just you."

WARRIORS RISING (JASON VAN CAMP)

On his second deployment to Iraq, Jason Van Camp was a detachment commander for an elite Special Forces unit, having trained for three years to earn his Green Beret. The Charted Territory of combat was brutal and unpredictable, but it was where Jason felt in control. The reach he had as a leader in the field was something he'd never experienced before. "It was as though I was a god. I mean, everybody did what I said. We had the air force, we had these unbelievable weapons, we had thousands of people under my command." At one point, Jason had 4,000 Kurds under his command on a mission to remove al-Qaeda from a local village. He recalls standing on his Humvee and looking out into the field, thinking, "This is like being Julius Caesar; this is unbelievable." But after three tours in Iraq in as many years, it was time for Jason to come home.

The Return to civilian life wasn't what Jason had envisioned. The autonomy and command he had in Iraq didn't carry over back home. Even routine trips to the grocery store would fill Jason with rage. "Why do I have to sit at this red light? Don't they know who I am?" While Jason admits there is a certain beauty about war, it still "hardens you as a person." The man who left was not the same man who came back. Prewar Jason was "happy-go-lucky, very bold," an open book with pages to be filled. Postwar Jason had chapters of his life he was desperately trying to forget. "You aren't as tolerant, you aren't as merciful, and you see how evil and dark and miserable the world is at times." It was a daily struggle to integrate what had happened to him in combat and make himself available to new Frontiers.

The onset of a seizure disorder pushed Jason out of the military for good with an honorable discharge. So he entered into an MBA program at BYU. Jason found himself in the middle of an entrepreneurial boom in Utah but felt out of place in the business world. "I'm from Virginia where nobody's an entrepreneur. Everybody works for the government." The further he progressed in his program, the same question kept coming up: "If I were to start a business, what would I do?" Instead of following the trend of internet-based startups, Jason marched to the beat of his own drum. Using his unique blend of military knowledge, his network of respected leaders, and his passion for sports, Jason drafted a business plan for a leadership consulting company. He wanted to bring his Special Forces brand of leadership to professional sports teams.

Jason's naivete worked in his favor as he crossed The Bridge into building a business. "Being young and dumb and bold and overconfident, I started cold-calling NFL teams. I went down the list alphabetically." Arizona Cardinals, Atlanta Falcons, Buffalo Bills, Carolina Panthers. No, no, no, and no. But Jason was undeterred, and halfway through the alphabet, he got his chance. "We finally got to the New York Jets, and I convinced them to give us a shot." After their presentation to the Jets team leadership, Jason and his team waited anxiously as head coach Rex Ryan and the general manager deliberated. Coach Ryan gave the verdict: "We've brought in similar types of companies who've been doing this for a while, but you guys blew us away. We're gonna hire you for the year." The company, Mission 6 Zero, had its first recruit.

The name Mission 6 Zero was chosen to honor Jason's past and to look toward the future. The "Mission," or the purpose, comes first and must align with your values. Jason was on a mission to do something meaningful with his life to honor the soldiers who had died under his command and didn't have the same chance. The number "6" refers to six o'clock, or a rear-facing direction, which is often the most vulnerable security position in combat. This represents the trust required for any team to function and was crucial for Jason as he invited partners into his new business. "That's where the power comes from in my business is the quality of people we have on the team." And last, "Zero," or true north on a magnetic compass. Zero symbolizes a forward push toward continual improvement, as well as a baseline for measuring progress. Jason's measure of progress has been highly influenced by his personal life. "Everything I do is for my wife and my daughter. I've learned more than anything, if you want to be successful in a marriage and with your family, you kind of surrender yourself in a way and you serve them."

Having gone full circle, from a veteran with a chip on his shoulder to a business owner with purpose, Jason is now able to be a Guide for other returning soldiers. Many of the instructors Jason uses for Mission 6 Zero training courses are injured combat veterans. As they prepared for clients, the conversation would regularly drift to the topic of contribution. These highly decorated veterans felt like they'd gone from a life of service to feeling like "charity cases." But Jason felt they weren't getting the hard feedback they needed. "These guys are military guys; I treat them like a brother. A lot of people don't know how to treat them, and it's a problem. You've got to hold them accountable; that's what they want. They don't want to be treated with kid gloves." Jason said if they wanted a mission, they needed to stand up and start working for it.

A commander at heart, Jason is leading the Allies who stood by him on the battlefield as they start their own ventures. With the founding of Warriors Rising, a nonprofit that helps veterans start or accelerate their businesses, Jason hopes to create the conditions to perpetuate the hiring of fellow American veterans. For those veterans willing to earn their future, he's ready to "empower them, to help give them a purpose again." Ultimately, Jason sees himself in every veteran struggling to make The Return from the battlefield. "It comes down to being humble and listening and connecting with the people around you. Just like in combat, you're thinking to yourself, 'I'm not gonna fail this guy to my right, this guy to my left, because I know sure as hell that he's not gonna fail me.'"

THE PERFECTION PIROUETTE (CHELSIE HIGHTOWER)

When Chelsie Hightower got a dancing dress for Easter and her five brothers got hockey sticks, she wasn't excited; she was devastated. She didn't want to dress up, and she didn't want to dance with the other little girls. When her mom tried to get her on stage at a recital, Chelsie made her feelings clear when she refused to move. "I had a stone-cold face, wouldn't move a muscle." It wasn't until she was nine years old that a ballroom dance program at her elementary school finally piqued her interest. "Something about ballroom struck me. It was the only elementary school in America at the time to have a ballroom program." Chelsie moved away from standing on the sidelines and stepped onto the dance floor of a new Frontier.

Chelsie struggled with self-doubt as she crossed The Bridge

into the world of dance. "I was that kid in class who was looking at everybody else, thinking, 'Why do they all know the steps and I don't know the steps? I can't get them.' I was so nervous." It didn't take long before she stopped looking around and started stepping forward. One day, it clicked: "It felt like something I'd been doing forever. It was a gift." At eleven years old, she was a national champion in ballroom. At fourteen, she was a sponsored dancer touring the country. At eighteen, Chelsie was standing in the audition room for the hit television show *So You Think You Can Dance?* She would go on to finish in the top six of the competition and was nominated for an Emmy for one of her routines.

From stage fright to center stage, Chelsie parlayed her success on *So You Think You Can Dance?* to become a lead dancer on another hit show, *Dancing with the Stars.* For seven seasons, Chelsie was under the bright lights of Hollywood. "This was in the height of my career. I was going to amazing movie premieres, parties, and interacting with some of the world's top talent on a daily basis." Chelsie even made the *Sports Illustrated* swimsuit issue with her dancing partner and bull rider, Ty Murray. At the top of the world, surrounded by people, Chelsie felt more alone than ever. She was ready to dance, but she felt unprepared for everything else. She was unprepared for the attention, unprepared for not being the best dancer in the room, and unprepared to deal with the pressure that had been building inside of her since she was eleven years old.

As a perfectionist, Chelsie thought she could keep her inner turmoil in check through sheer force of will. "If I could be mentally tough enough, everything's going to be okay." Chelsie was standing outside the Cave refusing to go in. "I couldn't accept that I couldn't control everything. It was this battle in my mind." Chelsie was afraid to admit she was out of control, to take on the inner work, and end her illusion of perfection. When her first panic attack arrived, it was clear she no longer had a choice. "I was fine one second and then I thought I was going to die. I was on my hands and knees in my room at 2:00 a.m. My whole body was shaking." She remembers feeling this "weight" sitting on top of her, a darkness coming over her. "It was scary because I didn't know how to be successful without this perfect world and this perfectly put-together thing."

When Chelsie's run on *Dancing with the Stars* ended after four years, it was the peak of her career and the valley of personal journey. "I was done. I was exhausted. Yet, I didn't know what to do. I was so stubborn in not wanting to give that up, the idea of perfection, because it felt good." But with the help of therapy, Chelsie began to make the treacherous trek down The Mountain and a **Return** to herself. "I finally got tired of running away from everything, dealing with all the pressure, and not dealing with it in a healthy way." The process of letting go of dance and letting go of her perfection was both release and recoil. "I never thought I would find myself in that situation, of feeling so lost because

I always knew who I was. I had such a strong sense of my purpose and what I wanted. Doors and opportunities were always opened." Chelsie's Return was slow and sometimes sideways. "I came from a background where every year I was growing, I was pushing, I was improving in dance, and I was one of the best at what I did. To take seven years to process my experiences and finally get to the point where I'm feeling like I'm on the other side has been incredibly frustrating and hard."

Chelsie feels the Reward is more about what we go through and what we struggle with than the highlight reels we collect along the way. The fame and magazine covers are only sustainable for so long until you have to face yourself. "Self-compassion, self-love, that is sustainable. You'll find more fulfillment in happiness and peace as opposed to pushing, trying to make your mark, and trying to prove you're good enough to everybody else. It's beautiful to be broken and to be humble. When you can say I'm good enough for myself. What I am is enough."

RETURNING MORE THAN YOU WERE

You have to make **The Return** on your journey or run the risk of becoming overconfident and suspending your growth. Descending from the heights of an exploration, you'll have the perspective to see you've become more than when you started. You are more than your money, more than your rank, more than your notoriety. And in the end, you are far more valuable to the world telling your story from the bottom of The Mountain than hiding at the top.

GET TRACTION

1. **Take a breather, but don't set up camp.** A long journey can be exhausting. Take the time to mend your wounds and recoup like Chelsie Hightower. The Return is a time of integration, reflecting, and preparing or repairing yourself for what's ahead. That said, be honest with yourself when it's time to get back on the road. Infinite reflection is another form of settling.

2. **You don't have to stand next to your art to prove you made it.** At a certain point, your business or art or kids need to function without you, but that doesn't mean you didn't have a huge hand in creating it. Imagine standing in a museum and holding up your painting to prove you made it instead of being back in your studio making more art. That's what I was doing with my business before I let my team step up. I was "holding up the art" when I should have been evolving my skillset and our business for the next step. Once the paint is dry, move on to the next canvas.

3. **What got you here won't get you there.** What got you to the top of one Mountain won't necessarily get you to the top of another. Although a commander on the battlefield, Jason Van Camp had to head back to the basic training of business school to build on the leadership and operational skills he already possessed. When you're making The Return, be humble and aware you're starting back at the bottom but with the strength and tools from your previous climbs.

4. **Remember what it took to get the base runners.** Grand slams can't happen without some base runners. After John Pestana sold his company for billions, he was overwhelmed by the pressure to produce again. He felt everyone was expecting him to hit another grand slam. But John had to remind himself of all the work it took to get those base runners. In his follow-up ventures, he knew he couldn't hit a grand slam until he put people on base.

The Return has given you a new perspective without a clouded view from the top. And with this newfound clarity, your focus will shift from yourself to the other. You'll feel the pull and the duty to be a Guide for those coming behind you.

<- CHAPTER 9 ->

FILLING IN THE MAP

"Bread shared isn't bread lost."

—SETH GODIN

Podcasting is not a money-making endeavor. In fact, breaking even means you're way above average. Creating the podcast that inspired this book was never about making money. I wanted to record the conversations I would have loved listening to when I was trying to figure out my path in life. It was also a gift to my friends and family, but to my utter delight, it has reached well beyond those circles. The letters and emails and social media posts I receive is what drives me to continue to pour my own time and personal resources into making it. Here are a few:

> "I found your podcast and I'm so inspired. I started listening about a month ago and I'm serious when I say it's one of the things I can't wait for each week."

"I have really appreciated listening to your podcast. So many of them have inspired me and I've decided to go back to school after 16 years to get my degree. I'm reading a lot more and I'm taking a coding class for fun."

"Wanted to say thanks for the inspiration. I've been trying to get my real estate license for two years and I'd taken the exam about four times and failed. I started getting motivated by your interviews and see you chase your dreams. I studied my heart out and finally yesterday I passed. Thanks for being there to motivate people and showing people it's a grind but it's worth it."

"Thanks for the podcast and for sharing your insight. I'm coming off my best year ever and it's easy to get complacent in that situation. The thought that someone 1 year, 2 years or even 5 or 10 years from now might REALLY NEED ME is insanely motivating. The idea of striving to be the absolute best version of myself in every way and every day so that I can be ready for that moment gives me goosebumps. Thank you."

I'm not including these for a personal ego boost but to show the impact you can have when you share generously about your explorations. In the Hero's Journey, this act is called Returning with the Elixir, or bringing back the magic potion. Generosity is magic. It makes the pie bigger and the world smaller. Generosity is what completes your journey. Your final task is to **Fill In The Map** and turn over your trail notes to the Explorers just setting out.

Filling in the Map marks the end of the cycle, but it isn't without its challenges. The role of Guide or "expert" can be a label you never feel quite qualified for. Maslow saw this as yet another danger we try to flee from: "To discover in oneself a great talent can certainly bring exhilaration but it also brings a fear of the dangers and responsibilities and duties of being a leader" [1]. Who am I to be a Guide? I barely made it back in one piece! But enhancing the map doesn't have to be a grand gesture; it's often a small moment. It's not how you share or how much; it's that you simply do it. You have the chance every day as a parent, as a coworker, as a human on this planet to share the tools and experience you've gathered along the way. You may be only one person in the world, but you can be the world to one person.

This last group of Explorers, although weary from the journey, felt the higher calling of giving back. They circled back to clear the path, to point out where they fell, and to put up lights in the darkest corners of their explored territories. They transformed themselves from seekers to Guides.

THE ULTIMATE FIGHT (COURT MCGEE)

When Court McGee was five years old, he got lost at an amusement park and was found that night hiding behind a garbage can. He was dehydrated, sick, and remained that way for weeks. "I didn't want to go to school. I was scared of crowds. I had some issues. So my parents put me in martial arts thinking it might help." He felt the calm come over him from the first class. Shin-Toshi karate proved to be the exact medicine Court needed: "I flourished. I loved it."

In junior high, Court made the switch from karate to wrestling and was on his way to being one of the top wrestlers in the state of Utah. Unfortunately, his success on the mat didn't translate to his social life. He was teased often but drew on his martial arts training of respect and restraint so he didn't fight back. But patience has its limits. In eighth grade gym class, while he was on the pull-up bar, some bullies pulled down Court's pants. Instead of coming to his aid, the coach laughed. Court was seething as his tormentors followed him into the locker room and broke his glasses. Enough was enough. "I smashed this kid's face into a locker, I punched a whole bunch of them, and then I took off running. I ended up coming back to get my glasses, and then got into it again." It was an awakening to both his strength and a newfound resolve not to back down.

Adding to Court's Road of Trials was his severe dyslexia. He wouldn't read a book cover to cover until he was twenty-five. Court cheated his way onto the honor roll so he could make the grades for college. His plan was simple: "I'll get a degree, and wrestling will provide that for me. Then I'll leave with the degree, work for thirty years, and retire." As simple as it sounded, the timing for Court's plan couldn't have been worse. Wrestling programs in Utah were shutting down, and the scholarships went with them. With no other viable options, Court attended a small state college but was quickly overwhelmed without the focus and drive of wrestling. A motorcycle accident added injury to insult as Court shattered his collarbone. The pain pills he received numbed more than his shoulder, and Court's path headed for a dark Frontier.

When the prescriptions ran out, Court looked for other ways to escape. "If you're getting pain pills from a guy, then he doesn't have any pills but he's got cocaine, you think, 'What's the difference?'" The arrests followed shortly after and the DUIs piled up. Court quit going to college and started selling cocaine. "I'm not a good drug dealer. I was using everything I could get my hands on." Court had a wake-up call when his longtime girlfriend, and the only stable thing in his life, walked out the door. "I thought of myself as this great person who was trying to figure out life, but I didn't know anything about the disease of addiction. I had no clue."

As his addiction took hold, Court lost his grip on the rest of his world. He tried to stop, but the train was moving too fast. The last stop was an overdose on heroin in a trailer park bathroom. The paramedics tried to revive Court on the way to the hospital, but he was pronounced dead on arrival. His story would have ended there if not for an astute narcotics officer who found the syringe he overdosed with.

He called the hospital and told them it was a heroin overdose. A lifesaving dose of naloxone was administered, and Court was put into a medically induced coma. After three relapses and countless "last times," Court found himself in his parents' basement on April 16, 2006. He had cracked a beer he'd stolen from his father when he heard footsteps on the stairs. He didn't try to hide it. Court's dad looked at him and calmly said, "Son, I thought you weren't supposed to drink." He knew he was done. It was the last drink or drug he ever had.

Four years later, Court was sitting in front of the producers of *The Ultimate Fighter*, a Fox Sports reality show and MMA competition. The winner of the competition would receive $50,000 and a contract with the UFC. Court had more than redemption riding on this opportunity; he had a baby on the way. Court had reconnected with his high school girlfriend, and they were expecting their first child. They were together but barely surviving. "I was at my breaking point. I wasn't in the UFC yet. I was working seventy to eighty hours a week. I was doing plumbing work on the side and selling knockoff clothes."

Court was selected for the show and began the fight for his life. "I put the work in, 4,000 hours, before I went into that damn house." Court won his first match but suffered a broken sternum in the process. Fighting through the pain and coming back from the brink of elimination, Court ended up winning the competition. When the media asked him how he planned to spend the money, most expected the stock answer of buying a big house or a new car. Court stunned them all by creating a personal endowment: "I'm going to pay myself two grand a month, and that's what I'm going to live off of." He was a man on a calculated mission.

A call from a narcotics officer a year later brought Court's story full circle. With five years sobriety and all his dues paid, Court worried he'd missed something along the way and was heading back to jail. The officer didn't want to lock him up; he wanted to lock him in as a speaker for an upcoming narcotics conference. *The Ultimate Fighter* had exposed the world to his rise from the ashes, and they wanted the impact to continue through education. When Court nervously took the stage for his speech, it was September 9, the anniversary date of his overdose. Sitting in the front row was the narcotics officer who saved his life.

Court has gone on to **Fill In The Map** for other struggling youth at conferences and schools across the nation through his nonprofit, The McGee Project. Looking up at the bleachers filled with teens, Court pictures himself and hopes he can give them the confidence to become "the person they never thought they could be." Court's ultimate message is as straightforward as he is: "I'm not that great of an athlete. I'm not that great of a speaker. But I'm the first guy at the gym and the last one to leave. That's why I've had success.

I put the time in." When kids come up to him after a speech and share their struggles with addiction, they can look to Court and see they've got a fighting chance.

WALK, RIDE, RODEO (AMBERLEY SNYDER)

When her family was planning a move from California to Utah, a seven-year-old Amberley Snyder informed her parents she would go only if she got a horse when they arrived. This would be a surprising request for most kids, but Amberley had been taking riding lessons since she was three years old. Amberley got her horse, but it came at a cost. After school one day, she asked her mom if she could play with a friend. Her mom said that was fine, but if her horse didn't get ridden every day, she couldn't enter the rodeo. Amberley didn't even hesitate. "If it came down to friends or rodeo, I'm going to rodeo. I made that decision."

Amberley crossed The Bridge into competitive barrel racing convinced of her path. "We were dedicated to what we did. At three years old, me and all my siblings knew what we wanted to do for the rest of our lives." Amberley's dad, the former Major League baseball player Cory Snyder, had always taught them about the tradeoffs necessary to be the best. "You didn't see anyone in my family going to parties in high school; you didn't see us doing kid things. We knew how to work hard, and we knew the formula to be successful. It takes sacrifice." The tradeoff culminated with a big Reward, as Amberley won the 2009 All-Around Cow-girl World Championship in the National Little Britches Rodeo Association.

Amberley was on top of the world when it all came crashing down. After a gas station stop on a trip to Denver, Amberley looked down to check her map, drifted into the other lane, and overcorrected. Her truck slid off the road and rolled seven times. She'd forgotten to fasten her seat belt after her stop. "I was ejected from the truck, hit a fence post, broke my back, and injured my spinal cord. I was sitting on the side of the road looking at my truck and realized I couldn't feel my legs. At eighteen, you don't expect your life to take a somersault like that." The accident had crushed Amberley's T12 vertebra, which left her paralyzed from the waist down. "You kind of live in this fantasy world for a bit. It's the stages of grief; first you go through denial. Even the hospital doesn't feel like the real world. You're like, okay, this is what I'm doing while I'm here. But when I get home, I'm gonna go back to how my life was before. The first day of therapy, the nurse asked me what my goals were, and I said, 'Walk, ride, rodeo.' That's it, plain and simple."

Life after the accident wasn't plain or simple, as the Road of Trials of recovery came into full view. With four months of rehab under her belt, Amberley wanted back on a horse. "That day was supposed to be super happy, but I was more sad than the day they told me I was never going to walk again." Through the hard days of rehab, she had convinced herself at least one part of her life would be the same. "But when I got back on a horse, I realized everything was different. I was devastated. I told my mom to sell my horses. I was done." Amberley went back to school and refocused on the basics of her new life. "I was hardheaded and stubborn and wanted to figure out life in a chair."

Amberley's Allies didn't sell her horses or let her give up on her dream. After eighteen months of taking it one day at a time, Amberley was back in the saddle with a new outlook on life. "There's a reason I had taken my seat belt off less than ten miles before. There's a reason I broke where I broke. There's a reason this is where I'm at, and the easiest thing to do is handle it on a daily basis. I let myself be mad and frustrated, but then I said, now what? What can I do with it?" What she did was work her way back to the pinnacle of her sport. With a custom saddle and more determination than ever, Amberley was voted in by fans to the largest and most lucrative rodeo in the world, The American. From the top of the Mountain, Amberley looked across at the 40,000 fans at AT&T Stadium in Dallas. "They could have voted in anyone in the world, and they picked me." She didn't win, but Amberley was only two tenths of a second behind the reigning world champion. She wasn't walking, but she was definitely riding and rodeoing.

Initially a reluctant Guide, Amberley has found a new passion in sharing her story. "I'm lucky by living my daily life, I give people strength. That's the crazy part, when people started leaning on my story or wanting me to speak, I'm like, man, I'm doing what you guys are doing; you just see my life as challenging. But I love speaking, and I never thought I would ever love anything as much as riding my horses."

In addition to public speaking, Amberley is **Filling in The Map** on the big and little screen. Her *Wheelchair Wednesdays* YouTube series attracts thousands of weekly viewers. "I'm the first paralyzed racer in the United States. People before me figured out how to ride, but they weren't competing. I was getting asked all the time, how are you doing this? And instead of writing out all these descriptions, I decided to make videos." Amberley's story went even bigger with the 2019 release of the Netflix movie *Walk, Ride, Rodeo*. "It's such a crazy thing that there's a movie. It was fun, stressful, exciting, and everything in between. It was also upsetting because you have to relive it." Amberley had only one non-negotiable for the movie—she would be the riding stunt double: "I'm the only one who does what I do."

PAYING IT FORWARD (RAND RASMUSSEN)

In twenty-four years as the head coach of the Bingham High School girls basketball team, Rand Rasmussen's record was

465 wins and 97 losses (thirty-eight shy of the all-time state record). His teams earned fourteen regional titles and four state championships. And in 2016, Rand was inducted into the Utah High School Sports Hall of Fame. But as a true servant leader, Rand was quick to give credit where credit was due: "I didn't score any points; I didn't get any rebounds. I might have pushed a button here and there, but that's pretty much it."

Coaching basketball was a bit unexpected given Rand's lifetime passion for baseball. "I was brought up in the hotbed of baseball in Southern California. In junior college, I got drafted in the sixth round and then later in the first round. I'm proud of that, but at the same time, that was forty years ago and about forty-five pounds ago." After a short stint in the minor leagues, Rand turned his focus to family life and coaching his son's Little League teams. Eventually, his aptitude and passion for coaching couldn't be ignored, and he made the commitment to **Fill in The Map** as a full-time coach. "I wanted to pay back the people who spent a lot of time shaping me when I was younger into who I became as a ballplayer and teacher."

As a Guide and leader, Rand knew preparation and practice were the most critical parts of any endeavor. "The highlight to me is going to practice every day. The games are over in thirty-two minutes. It's no big deal. Practice is where you see the growth in the kids" [2]. In addition to coaching girls basketball, Rand was also the assistant boys baseball coach for one of the most successful programs in the country. Their scouting reports on opposing teams went well beyond the ordinary. "We're always looking for the advantage, always doing our homework. It's like any business, paying attention to all those little minute details; you don't leave anything to chance."

To successfully develop his players, Rand was careful to keep his distance. "People try to be too close with their kids or their players. I was not put on earth to be my son's best friend. I was put on earth to be their mentor and their father." Rand had a reputation of being tough, but it was always in the service of making his students and players better. "Kids don't have a problem with being disciplined or called out. They have a problem when you have favorites. I tell them the first day I don't have favorites; you're all going to be treated the same." Rand's respect and fairness translated into results when the game was on the line. "If I say, 'We need to go through that brick wall to win,' my kids are going to figure out a way to get through that brick wall. When you treat them fairly and they know that you love them at all costs, you can say what you need to and they'll be fine." Rand kept an arm's length with parents as well. "I have to make tough decisions all the time, and it makes it more difficult when you're friends with that parent. After they've graduated, then I go out to dinner with them."

The hardest part about coaching wasn't losing but when Rand had to say goodbye to his seniors. "My worst moments happen once a year. When it gets down to the end and I've got to talk about these seniors, I can't even speak. I've had years with those girls; they're like my own daughters." When they walked out the door, he hoped at least some of them would become Guides as well. "They don't have to give me anything at the end of the season; I don't care about that. What I want is for them to pay it forward and be teachers for the next generation of kids coming up." Rand clearly had an impact, as eleven of the girls he coached have gone on to be high school coaches.

In 2013, Rand was the one saying goodbye to his basketball team. A few years later, he bade farewell to the baseball team. A cancer diagnosis shifted his focus from the field to family. Coaching had kept him from being the grandfather and husband he felt he needed to be. "I thought about my wife. For thirty-seven years, she's been at home as I'm trying to help these kids get prepared. She means absolutely everything to me, and that's why I resigned." Rand would need the strength of his family and an unsuspecting coach to get through his twenty-eight chemotherapy treatments. "There are days where you curl up in the fetal position. On one of my last treatments, I had a bad day. I felt like, 'Why me?' And then this voice behind me yells, 'Hey, Rand!' It was Trina; she had no hair and she was four years old. She said, 'I've only got eighteen more chemotherapy treatments!' I've not gotten in the fetal position since that day. If that little one can do it, I'm going to do it. So I handle every day as it comes along."

Before Rand left this earthly life, I had the chance to visit him one last time. To see the love in his eyes and know our friendship was as special to him as it was to me is something I'll never forget. Rand, I'm sorry we never got to Duke for a basketball game, but I'm so grateful for all the adventures we did have. You took a chance on a kid you didn't have to, and you played a critical role in my life that I needed. I'm proud to have known you and call you a dear friend. Your legacy lives on in the thousands of lives you touched and the lives all of us will continue to touch. And if you ever look down and see I've veered off my path, please tell me in your own way to straighten my damn hat.

Love you, Rand.

FILLING IN THE MAP EXTENDS THE REWARD

When you give generously, when you Fill in the Map, you're completing the loop of your journey and lighting the path for someone else. The feeling you get when you help someone on their own journey is what will propel you past the discomfort of starting something new for yourself. As Carl Sagan put it, "For small creatures such as we, the vastness is bearable only through love" [3]. Filling in the Map isn't an act of self-aggrandizement, a "look what I've done" showcase, but an act of love. It's the difference between building a road and building a monument. Monuments crumble; roads last.

GET TRACTION

1. **Talk to your younger self.** When it comes time to shift gears from doing to guiding, you might struggle to know what to share. Court McGee felt like he didn't have anything to say until he thought about talking to his younger self. That was the spark he needed for the McGee Project and why he gives his time looking eye to eye with high schoolers across the country. Somewhere in the world right now is the younger version of yourself. They'll have a different name, but they're about to embark on the journey you just took. What would you tell them?

2. **Your ordinary is extraordinary.** Because your journey was made up of a thousand tiny steps, the achievement will seem commonplace to you. But an ordinary day for someone like Amberley Snyder is an extraordinary feat for someone starting out. No matter how unremarkable your story feels, telling people how you got there will make a mark.

3. **Inspire the next generation of Guides.** Filling in The Map isn't only about teaching but also inspiring those who should teach. Rand Rasmussen may have built championship teams, but his ultimate goal was to motivate his players to be generous coaches themselves. Share the lesson *and* the lesson plans.

And then it's done. The long journey has come full circle. Bridges crossed, rough roads traveled, and mountains climbed. You're back safe and sound. Time to settle down and...

Ha, get up! It's time to C.H.A.R.T. your next path.

CONCLUSION

THE JOURNEY STARTS ANEW

"I live my life in widening circles
that reach out across the world.
I may not complete this last one
but I give myself to it."

—RAINER MARIA RILKE, *BOOK OF*
HOURS: LOVE POEMS TO GOD

Did you know houseboats don't have a bilge pump in the front? Me neither. I found out the hard way (as usual) at one of my favorite places in the world, Lake Powell. Not long after getting a new boat, I planned a huge trip with dozens of people. I was loaded with a week's worth of supplies, so I wasn't worried when I noticed the boat sitting a bit low in the water. It's also not unusual for water to come up on the front of the boat as you hit a wake or pick up speed. But as we got farther away from the dock, the water coming onto the boat wasn't splashing—it was staying. Things went from bad to worse when a wave from a passing cruise boat flooded the front deck and turned the bedroom below it into an unplanned waterbed. We weren't sitting low; we were sinking.

Without hesitation, I swung the boat around and got everyone onto another boat traveling with us. There was nowhere to safely beach and wait for help, so I radioed the Coast Guard and started heading back. I could see the boat sinking under my feet as bigger and bigger waves crashed over the front. The captain, as they say, was going down with his ship. As it was reported later on the local news, the Coast Guard said I had naively saved the boat by moving forward. It didn't feel naive to me; what other choice did I have? You're either moving forward or you're sinking (settling) to the bottom. That's the life of an Explorer—movement. When one Frontier has been mapped, it's time to move on to the next adventure. The joy of the Explorer comes from the endless progress toward an unmet potential, unencumbered by the anchor of what's already been done. As Campbell puts it, "The self is the whole range of possibilities that you've never even thought of. If all you know about yourself is what you found out about yourself, well, that already happened" [1].

Embracing the eternal cycle of change, and giving yourself

to it, is an inexhaustible well of identity and purpose. As an Explorer, you charge through the lows to the Reward on the horizon. At the top, you take time to breathe and enjoy the view, but you don't linger too long so you can head back down and share what you've learned. You're either exploring new territory in an act of constant regeneration, or you're settling. There is no in between. Yet, embracing the identity of the Explorer isn't easy. Right when you've got it all figured out, it's time to lose yourself again. You'll have to pull away from the comfort, from your carefully honed expertise and become a novice once again. But you're a novice with miles under your belt. Your mental models of what's possible have expanded. There is Maslow-like "delight" in your newness.

You are no different than the Explorers I've highlighted in this book. They have hang-ups and fears and hardships as we all have, yet they push through them to **C.H.A.R.T.** their own course. They **C**hanged Their Minds, **A**dapted their Bodies, **R**evealed their Hearts, and **T**ransmitted their Souls into the work of their lives. Their identities weren't tied to promotions or a prevailing culture but to personal progress and cultivating curiosity.

Like a tree, building upon itself each year from a sapling to a towering oak, so will you form the trunk of your life on your explorations. Your skills and network and confidence will grow around that strong base. And the slim branches that could barely support your own needs in the beginning will be solidified and provide for those around you. They'll reach out and support your Allies, support the causes you care about, and provide the seeds for those yet to come. The legacy and impact of your findings will last beyond your final exploration. The updated maps, the Threshold Guardians outwitted, and the earth you pack down into a well-worn path will remain.

So here we are again, two potential paths.

PATH ONE

You turn the last page of this book and toss it onto your growing pile of self-help books. You thought of a few things you might explore as you read, but are they realistic? A little Settler climbs onto your shoulder and whispers in your ear, "What if your ideas aren't any good? What if they're too hard? What if you fail?" One by one, you close yourself off to these new paths before you've stepped a foot down any of them. You settle back onto the couch, back into your life, because it's not that bad, right? Maybe you'll explore tomorrow.

PATH TWO

You turn the last page of this book and quickly flip back to the notes you've taken in the margins. So many ideas! A little Explorer climbs onto your shoulder and whispers in your ear, "All the good journeys aren't taken; you just have to take the first step. Let yourself be drawn toward new Frontiers, and open yourself to the path. Exploring your life can begin today." A sense of ease fills your body because there isn't "ahead" or "behind" on the Explorer's path—only the forward progress you choose to make. You stand, knowing with every fiber of your being that when you come to your final day and the person you've become meets the person you could have been, they'll look the same.

Where are you heading?

ACKNOWLEDGMENTS

JIMMY

When I was a little kid, I always knew I wanted to live a big life. To "have money and a cool job." I wanted to be "successful," I guess you could say. I didn't know what that meant or what it looked like, but I knew I wanted it. Problem is, when you are first starting down the path, you don't really know how far it goes. You don't know the obstacles that await, and you don't know how long you'll wander before you start to see any of that success.

It's so important to look for mentors along the way and Guides to help us. They are the cheerleaders of the race who tell us to keep going, who promise us we're on the right path and that we're winning. They help us push through the pain of the race knowing that the Reward will be worth it in the end.

In my life, I've had so many mentors who have helped me along the way. So many fans and so many "helpers" who encouraged me to keep going, to be myself, and to take the next step. I wouldn't be doing this book justice if I didn't acknowledge several of them. But this book is especially dedicated to my late friend Rand Rasmussen, who is highlighted in this book. A few months ago, Rand passed away after his long battle with cancer. A few days before he passed, I had one last chance to fly up to Portland and see him. He had a special look in his eyes, and I saw pure love. I knew he was proud of me. Rand always loved following my crazy adventures, and I loved knowing he appreciated me exactly as I am. I miss my friend, but I'm glad to know he gets to join me on all of my adventures now.

I also want to give a special thanks to my life coach and close friend Melissa Perdue. It was through her guidance and love that I was able to quit shaming myself and start to love this beautiful man that I am. She knows all my doubts and fears, all my failures, including the ones I never shared with anyone else. And yet she just loved. She saw me before anyone else did. Thank you for your love and thank you for your guidance. I try and live my life as a testimony to you and your work with me, knowing you don't need me to be anything but proud of what we are accomplishing as we keep pushing forward on this path we call life. So as my guide and someone who helped me see the light when it was really dark, thank you. This book is a compilation of all the lessons you taught me that I now get to pass on to others. I have so much love and honor for you.

Thank you,
Jimmy

A small and very incomplete list of important mentors and friends in my life:

Bill Pipes
Rand Rasmussen
My parents and siblings
President Ballard
President Hammond
Mike Ferry
Nancy Auge
Ron Meeker
Shaun Michael
Paul Hutchinson
Andrew McCubbins
Cameron Carling

CAMERON

In seventh grade, a new student joined our Honors English class a few weeks into the school year. He didn't quite fit the mold. Most of his words avoided the page and ended up as verbal arguments with our exasperated teacher. When I was assigned to help him come up with a story that wasn't about baseball, he flatly refused. As a rule follower, I was shocked. As a teenager trying to find his way, I was intrigued.

Twenty-five years later, Jimmy Rex is still shocking and intriguing me. He explores more in a weekend than most people hope to tackle in a lifetime. So when I had a mid-life cris...er... sabbatical, Jimmy was the first person I called on. I knew I needed to write. Something. I asked Jimmy if he needed any copywriting for his business to get my engines going. He said, "Let's write a book together instead."

Thank you, Jimmy, for not letting me settle. For pushing me into this new Frontier and being a Guide, Ally, and the ultimate destroyer of Threshold Guardians along the way. You're a magnet and a boundary pusher and the most generous person I've ever met. I'd go with you into the thickest jungle (you first, though).

To Mrs. Whipple, the seventh-grade English teacher whom Jimmy tormented, thank you. Not for giving me the impossible task of changing Jimmy's mind but for inspiring me to write. You gave me permission to be poetic, to be bold, and to embrace that writing is, and always will be, the act of rewriting.

Thank you, Costa Rica, for being so boring and beautiful

I had no other choice but to stare at the ocean and help write this book.

To my mom and dad. Where to start? Thank you for giving me life, for giving me love, and for always being my number one fan. Mom, thank you for taking a fine-toothed comb to every inch of this book. You took out the rocks that allowed it to flow. Dad, thank you for showing me what hard work looks like. I wouldn't have had the discipline to do this without you.

And to my wife, Marcella, a thank-you doesn't seem like enough. When we crossed our bridge together in Brooklyn all those years ago, I knew I'd found the perfect companion. You've always stood by me, even when I didn't realize I was keeping you at arm's length. We've seen some dark caves and many more great heights, and it feels like the journey has just begun. Thank you for fixing the introduction by telling me the hard truth (as you always do). Te amo.

Cameron

APPENDIX

ADDITIONAL RESOURCES
THE PODCAST

(www.thejimmyrexshow.com)

The Jimmy Rex Show is a collection of over 200 interviews highlighting modern-day Explorers building exceptional lives. From professional athletes to entrepreneurs to cultural thought leaders, each guest shares their unique path to a life well lived.

THE SOCIAL REALTOR COACHING COURSE

(https://www.mrjimmyrex.com/)

I've spent over $500,000 on coaches and learning techniques to get better at real estate, pushing myself to be the person my younger self had no clue how to be. I had to claw myself out of massive debt, make it through the largest real estate crisis in history, and learn how to run and lead a profitable business. And I did it all the hard way. But you shouldn't have to.

I started a coaching program for real estate agents to share the most important lessons I learned, which led me to selling over 300 homes a year. I am forever thankful for the numerous mentors who taught and guided me along my journey. With my course, I hope to pay it forward and be a guide to others.

REFERENCES

INTRODUCTION

1. Rex, Jimmy. "The Jimmy Rex Show." 2019. http://thejimmyrexshow.com/
2. Maslow, Abraham. *Toward a Psychology of Being.* Floyd, VA: Sublime Books, 2014.
3. Maslow, Abraham. *The Farther Reaches of Human Nature.* New York: Penguin, 1993.
4. Campbell, Joseph. *The Power of Myth.* New York: Doubleday, 1988.
5. Korzybski, Alfred. "A Non-Aristotelian System and Its Necessity for Rigour in Mathematics and Physics." In *Science and Sanity*, pp. 747–761. Forest Hills, NY: Institute of General Semantics, 1931.

CHAPTER 1: ORDINARY WORLD

1. Campbell, Joseph. *The Hero's Journey: Joseph Campbell on His Life and Work* (The Collected Works of Joseph Campbell). Novato, CA: New World Library, 2003.

CHAPTER 2: FACING THE FRONTIER

1. Campbell, Joseph. *The Hero with a Thousand Faces.* p. 42. Novato, CA: New World Library, 2008.
2. Campbell, Joseph. *The Hero with a Thousand Faces.* p. 43. Novato, CA: New World Library, 2008.
3. Fields, Jonathan. "Superimposed Limitations..." Good Life Project, mailing list, July 11, 2019.
4. Ballard, Katherine. "Tim Ballard's Wife, Katherine." OUR Stories, September 2014. http://ourrescue.org/blog/beside-every-good-man/

CHAPTER 3: CROSSING THE BRIDGE

1. Gilbert, Elizabeth. "Elizabeth Gilbert Shows Up for... Everything." Interview by Chris Anderson, The TED Interview, October 2018. https://www.ted.com/talks/the_ted_interview_elizabeth_gilbert_shows_up_for_everything?language=en
2. Pressfield, Steven. *The War of Art: Break through the Blocks and Win Your Inner Creative Battles.* New York: Black Irish Entertainment, 2002.

3. Campbell, Joseph. *The Power of Myth*. New York: Doubleday, 1988.

CHAPTER 4: THE ROAD OF TRIALS

1. Campbell, Joseph. *Sukhavati: Place of Bliss: A Mythic Journey with Joseph Campbell*. DVD. Acorn Media. 2007.
2. Maslow, Abraham. *Toward a Psychology of Being*. p. 52. Floyd, VA: Sublime Books, 2014.

CHAPTER 5: THE CAVE

1. Campbell, Joseph. *The Hero's Journey: Joseph Campbell on His Life and Work* (The Collected Works of Joseph Campbell). p. 61. Novato, CA: New World Library, 2003.
2. Campbell, Joseph. *The Hero with a Thousand Faces*. p. 136. Novato, CA: New World Library, 2008.
3. Waterboys. "Conquering Kili." https://waterboys.org/kili/

CHAPTER 7: THE REWARD

1. Skotko, Brian G., Susan P. Levine, Eric A. Macklin, and Richard D. Goldstein. "Family Perspectives about Down Syndrome." *American Journal of Medical Genetics Part A* 170A, no. 4 (2016): 930-941.

2. Brown, Brené. "The Anatomy of Trust." Oprah's Supersoul Sessions, July 2019. https://www.youtube.com/watch?v=HX7pxiwzSzQ

CHAPTER 9: FILLING IN THE MAP

1. Maslow, Abraham. *Toward a Psychology of Being.* p. 59. Floyd, VA: Sublime Books, 2014.
2. Donaldson, Amy. "Bingham's Rand Rasmussen Retires after 24 Years at Helm of Girls Basketball Team." *Deseret News*, March 1, 2013.
3. Sagan, Carl. *Contact.* p. 430. New York: Gallery Books, 1985.

CONCLUSION

1. Campbell, Joseph. *The Hero with a Thousand Faces.* p. 263. Novato, CA: New World Library, 2008.

FEATURED CONTACTS
MIRANDA ALCARAZ

Twitter: @AlcarazMirandaB
Instagram: @fearlessmiranda
Website: streetparking.com

TIM BALLARD

Twitter: @timballard
Instagram: @timballard89
Website: ourrescue.org

DAN CLARK

danclark.com
Twitter: @danclarkspeak
Facebook: facebook.com/danclarkspeak

JANE ANN CRAIG

Instagram: @cjaneann
Website: janeanncraig.com

HAL ELROD

Twitter: @HalElrod
Instagram: @hal_elrod
Website: halelrod.com

JIMMER FREDETTE

Twitter: @jimmerfredette
Instagram: @jimmerfredette_32
Website: jimmerosity.org

SETEMA GALI

Twitter: @SetemaGali
Instagram: @SetemaGali
Website: setemagali.com

GARRETT GEE

Twitter: @garrettgee
Instagram: @garrettgee
Website: garrettg.ee

JASON HEWLETT

Twitter: @jasonhewlett
Instagram: @jasonhewlett
Website: jasonhewlett.com

CHELSIE HIGHTOWER

Twitter: @chelsiehightowr
Instagram: @chelshightower
Website: chelsiehightowerdance.com

BRAD JENSEN

Twitter: @thesoberbuilder
Instagram: @thesoberbodybuilder
Website: keynutrition.com

JAMES LAWRENCE

Twitter: @IronCowboyJames
Instagram: @ironcowboyjames
Website: ironcowboy.com

KYLE MAYNARD

Twitter: @kylemaynard
Instagram: @kylemaynard
Website: kyle-maynard.com

COURT MCGEE

Twitter: @Court_McGee
Instagram: @courtmcgeemma
Website: mcgeeproject.org

TREVOR MILTON

Twitter: @nikolatrevor
Instagram: @lakepowelltrevor
Website: nikolamotor.com

JOHN PESTANA

Twitter: @jpestana
Instagram: @johnpestana
Website: observepoint.com

SUSAN PETERSEN

Instagram: @susan.m.petersen
Website: freshlypicked.com

OAKLEY PETERSON

Twitter: @NothingdownAI
Instagram: @nothingdownaboutit
Website: nothingdownaboutit.com

JUSTIN PRINCE

Twitter: @justinkprince
Instagram: @iamjustinprince
Website: iamjustinprince.com

CLINT PULVER

Instagram: @clintpulver
Website: clintpulver.com

RAND RASMUSSEN—IN MEMORIAM

https://www.linkedin.com/pulse/fix-your-damn-hat-tribute-my-friend-rand-rasmussen-jimmy-rex/

JORDAN ROMERO

Twitter: @JordanForNepal
Instagram: @gordybones
Website: jordan-romero.com

HAYSAM SAKAR

Instagram: @haysamsakar
Website: 24motors.com

JASON SISNEROS

Instagram: @therealjasonsisneros
Website: jasonsisneros.com

ANDREW SMITH

Twitter: @andrewk_smith
Instagram: @andrewksmith
Website: fourfoodsgroup.com

AMBERLEY SNYDER

Twitter: @SnyderAmberley
Instagram: @amberleysnyder
Website: amberleysnyder.org

JASON VAN CAMP

Twitter: @jasonbavancamp
Instagram: @jasonbavancamp
Website: warriorrising.org

KYLE VAN NOY

Twitter: @KVN_03
Instagram: @realkylevannoy
Website: vannoyvalorfoundation.org

BAYA VOCE

Twitter: @baya_voce
Instagram: @baya_voce
Website: bayavoce.com

LACY WEST

Twitter: @LacedHair
Instagram: @lacygadegaard
Website: lacedhair.com

SEAN WHALEN

Twitter: @Sean_Whalen
Instagram: @seanwwhalen
Website: seanwhalen.com

ABOUT THE AUTHORS

JIMMY REX is best known for his fifteen-year career in real estate. With more than 2,200 homes sold, he closed Utah's most expensive home sale in history at $32.5 million. He's coached more than 1,500 agents, authored the best-selling book *Next Wave of Influence in Real Estate*, and is the creator and host of the popular podcast *The Jimmy Rex Show*.

CAMERON CARLING earned his BA in communication studies from UCLA and is currently an operations manager for Google's IT department. Here, he's spent more than a decade leading technical support and user experience teams and co-developing an industry-leading IT training program.

Made in the USA
Middletown, DE
13 January 2022

58573647R00154